T0114296

Praise for
Everything Happens for a Reason

"Skillful, intelligent, and effective."

—*Healing Lifestyles and Spas*

"This well-written self-help guide by psychologist Kirshenbaum . . . [includes] a wealth of advice, such as a seven-step method to overcome fear and a list of the ten elements of true love."

—*Publishers Weekly*

"Mira Kirshenbaum mesmerizingly interweaves personal narratives with psychological wisdom. *Everything Happens for a Reason* is a transforming book for all who struggle with accidents of fate and how to make lemonade out of lemons when confronted with meaningless suffering. This book is a compelling guide for each reader to find a unique way to begin life anew after a tragedy."

—Eva Fogelman, author of *Conscience and Courage:*
Rescuers of Jews During the Holocaust

"Mira Kirshenbaum is able to lead the reader of her new book, just like her many patients, on the path of interior truth and peace. I strongly recommend her book, which should appeal to all of us."

—Guy G. Stroumsa, founding director, Center for the
Study of Christianity, the Hebrew University of Jerusalem

"Once again, Dr. Mira Kirshenbaum has written a book of timely importance. This beautiful book teaches us how to accept the course of our lives, become more resilient and less fearful in the face of change. All those interested in living with passion rather than with regret should read this most insightful book."

—Arthur P. Ciaramicoli, Ed.D., Ph.D., author of
Performance Addiction

"I found Mira Kirshenbaum's book *Everything Happens for a Reason* accessible, and full of life-giving spirit. She tackles life's most challenging and existential issues with a rare combination of authority, gentleness, and humility, and provides practical insights that will move the reader toward greater healing and wholeness. I will be recommending this book to friends and clients alike, and am glad to have it in my own library for reference."

—Dr. Ross Porter, clinical psychologist, founder of
Stillpoint Resources, and author of *To Kindle a Fire* and *Hidden Graces*

"Mira Kirshenbaum describes herself as practical, but filled with dreams. In this book she helps make dreams a reality by looking at the traps we fall into when things go wrong. Her years of brass-tacks experience will help you see your life differently and allow you to rise to new heights in your private life, your love life, your career. Invaluable wisdom!"

—Arthur Rosenfeld, author of *The Truth About Chronic Pain*

"Brilliant, beautiful, and bound to make a profound difference in all of our lives! With her warm voice and wise prose, Mira helps us discover the deeper meaning of the most challenging events. In these insightful pages, you'll not only find the closure you need, but the hidden meaning of your life."

—Debra Waterhouse, M.P.H., R.D., bestselling author of
Outsmarting Female Fatigue

"Mira Kirshenbaum's *Everything Happens for a Reason* is one of life's wonderful surprises. Insightful, wise, and warm, the book can help us all find the often elusive reasons behind seminal events in our lives. I walked away from this book with courage, curiosity, and a sense of peace about my own life's challenges—past, present and future."

—Mary J. Shomon, bestselling author of
Living Well with Hypothyroidism

"The search for meaning is perhaps the most definitive aspect of our humanness. *Everything Happens for a Reason* offers the reader an easy and thoughtful hand in this oh-so-important quest. Mira Kirshenbaum is a wise and seasoned guide, her book a welcome map of the difficult terrain of life."

—Dr. Dorothy Firman, coauthor of
Chicken Soup for the Mother and Daughter Soul

Finding the

True Meaning

of the

Events

in Our Lives

Everything Happens for a Reason

MIRA KIRSHENBAUM

Three Rivers Press • New York

Copyright © 2004 by Mira Kirshenbaum

All rights reserved.

Published in the United States by Three Rivers Press, an imprint of the Crown
Publishing Group, a division of Random House, Inc., New York.
www.crownpublishing.com

Three Rivers Press and the Tugboat design are registered trademarks of Random
House, Inc.

Originally published in hardcover in the United States by Harmony Books, an
imprint of the Crown Publishing Group, a division of Random House, Inc., New
York, in 2004.

DESIGN BY ELINA D. NUDELMAN

Library of Congress Cataloging-in-Publication Data
Kirshenbaum, Mira.
Everything happens for a reason : finding the true meaning of the events in our lives
/ Mira Kirshenbaum.
p. cm.
1. Life change events—Psychological aspects. 2. Meaning (Psychology) 3. Conduct
of life. I. Title.
BF637.L53K57 2004
158—dc22   2003021259

ISBN 978-1-4000-8321-3

First Paperback Edition

To Shaye

Acknowledgments

My entire life now has been embraced by people struggling to find meaning for the events in their lives.

I must have started doing "research" for this book when I was four years old. There I was in a displaced persons' camp in the American Zone in postwar Germany, surrounded by survivors of the worst experiences you can imagine. No one confided in me back then, of course, but no one would have stopped talking either when this tiny blond girl clutching her doll wandered near their conversations. And who knows how often I heard people argue about whether the things that had happened to them could have any meaning? Who knows how often I heard their tears of despair or sighs of hope?

And then just yesterday on the radio I heard an American soldier who'd lost a limb in the fighting in Iraq say, "You can never know why anything happens." But I could also hear in his voice a hunger for meaning that I must've heard in all the voices around me back when I was a small child.

It's people like this that I want to thank for making this book possible. It was their hunger for meaning that inspired me. And it was my hunger, too.

There's another group of men and women who went beyond the unanswered question *Why?* They pressed forward and *discovered* the reason that some big event happened to them. The people who did this are my heroes, and they are the ones I have to thank most of all for this book. It's filled with their stories, but they gave me enough material to fill a dozen books. Without their help and inspiration this would not have been possible.

I need to thank my husband and partner, Dr. Charles Foster, for writing and researching this book with me. Every idea, every word here is as much his as it is mine.

My mother made heroic sacrifices for me, and as I've learned more and more of our story I realize that she saved my life a number of times. She's had a huge impact on me and on this book. I can't begin to express my gratitude. Many thanks also to my brother and sister-in-law.

I'm incredibly grateful to my children for their help, support, and encouragement.

My agent, Howard Morhaim, is also my friend, my adviser, and my all-around guru, and I'm very thankful to him for everything.

A very special thanks to my publisher and editor, Shaye Areheart. I've known Shaye for twenty years. At strategic points she's come through for me big-time. The way this book looks and reads is very much the result of Shaye's genius and passion.

Thanks also to Jeanne Forte, who worked so hard with Shaye on this book. And thanks to Sibylle Kazeroid, my smart production editor.

Julie Will has impressed me with her energy and ability. Thanks.

I very much want to thank Debbie Natoli and Mary Shuck for creating what is quite simply the best book cover I've ever seen.

I'm incredibly grateful to Katherine Beitner and Melissa Kaplan for their wonderful work in bringing this book to people's attention.

Finally, much thanks to all the people who've reached out to me over the years. Your suggestions, your requests for help, and your expressions of appreciation have very much formed the fabric of my life.

In a dark time, the eye begins to see.

~Theodore Roethke

Happy is the person who can know the reasons for things.

~Virgil

Nothing is too wonderful to be true.

~Michael Faraday

Contents

To My Readers

I hope this book will have an impact on your life, but I know that it has completely changed my life.

When I started actively doing the research on which this book is based I didn't believe in God. I'd been very religious until I became a teenager, and then suddenly I lost whatever it was that made it possible for me to have faith. You hear about people who wake up one morning and find they've lost their sense of taste. I lost my sense of God. And it was gone for most of my adult life.

I can't really say how it happened that I've completely regained my faith in God, my utter sense that He is real and always with me. All I know is this: I heard story after story of people who'd gone through something incredibly difficult and then almost miraculously discovered real meaning in what they'd gone through. And somehow in the process of hearing how life is filled with meaning I became filled with the presence of God.

Don't misunderstand me. This is not a book about God. It's a book about people and their search for meaning. You don't need to believe in God to believe that there's meaning in the events of your life. Plenty of the people you'll meet in these pages who discovered the reason they went through something are not believers. And that's fine.

But this *is* a book about how everything can change for the better when you see that *all* of the events of your life have meaning and value. Things will probably change for you in a way that's different from the way they changed for me. The point is that there are things we desperately need if we're going to take the next steps in our life, and somehow discovering how everything has meaning gives us just what we need to take those steps.

All I can promise you is that by the end of this book you'll have found the meaning of the events of your life. But I'm sure this knowledge will have a profound effect on you and on how you live. I hope you will visit me at www.EverythingHappens ForAReason.org and let me know about it. I look forward to hearing from you.

part 1

Why Everything Happens

Everything *Really Does* Happen for a Reason

———◆◆◆———

Is it really true that everything happens for a reason? After all, that's an amazing thing to say—that no matter what happens to you, not only does something valuable come out of it but it's just what you need.

Amazing as it sounds, it *is* true. It's taken me a long time, but I now see that even in the worst disaster—and I've had my share—there are wonderful gifts, hidden opportunities, or life-enhancing lessons. And we couldn't have gotten them any other way. If someone as hardheaded as I am can come to understand this, anyone can.

Of course, sometimes it's easy for us to believe that everything happens for a reason. We see it in little ways, like when our plans for an evening out fall through at the last minute, and we discover that everything we really want is at home that night anyway.

And sometimes we see it in not-so-little ways. A woman I know wrenched her back and had to spend a month in bed. She felt this was the last thing she needed in her life, particularly since it happened at a time when she had to make some important decisions. And then it hit her—this was *exactly* what she needed. Her old habit had been to rush impetuously into a new decision without thinking it through. Now it was as if life were saying, "If you won't give yourself time to think, I will."

We very much *want* to believe that the things that happen to us have great meaning. It's the way we feel life should be. Yes, some days we feel our life's a soap opera. But we want—we *need*—to have the sense that there's a purpose and value to it all. And we're right.

I want to reassure you: When you discover the true meaning of the events in your life, everything changes.

You feel stronger because your sense that everything has meaning gives you great confidence.

You feel wiser because you see how everything connects.

You're more in touch with who you are because you know that you're living the life you were meant to lead.

And you're happier because you're able to put your loss behind you and have a sense of a future filled with good things.

Until you get to this place, nothing is going to feel right. Let's say you're outdoors and you suddenly feel a drop of moisture fall on your head. You're not going to be able to think of anything else until you figure out why that happened. Is water dripping from some air conditioner up high? Is it starting to rain? Is a flying monkey peeing on your head? *You have to know why that drop of moisture fell on your head because you can't feel safe going forward until you do.*

We need to know why much more when what fell on our heads is a catastrophe. If you can't make sense of the catastrophe, it's as if your life is mere dice on a crap table—if nothing has any meaning, everything's random, anything can happen.

It's painful to live not knowing why you got so sick that time or why you lost the love of your life—much more painful than people suspect. One woman I know was flying home for Thanksgiving when she was in college. As the plane was flying along twenty thousand feet in the air, she developed a terrible earache. But that's not what made her cry. In the dark of a nighttime flight she was sobbing because there *was* pain like this in the world, seemingly without any rhyme or reason.

One guy described this feeling differently: "When I think about the bad stuff that's happened in my life, I feel I'm just a goddamn fool of the cosmos. It's humiliating! On a sidewalk crowded with people, *I'm* the one who's stepped in the dog poop. No one else is as stupid or unlucky as I am. The problem is: How can I go forward, how can I trust the future if I feel I am this stupid unlucky guy?"

Knowing that there's a reason for what happens also saves us from being filled with blame. Blame is a very human attempt to make sense of some catastrophe, but most of the time we hate the way it feels. And yet when something bad happens to us, it's almost a reflex to think, *It's because everyone hates me, because I'm a loser, because I'm doomed.* And so the blame begins.

We blame other people, and then we end up with the sense that the world is full of bad people. We blame ourselves, and then instead of feeling healthy, strong, and whole we see ourselves as sick, weak, and broken. And we blame life itself. What could be more demoralizing than feeling condemned to having bad things always happen to us and not being able to do anything about it?

Blame is like a boomerang that loops around and bonks us on the noggin. Try this yourself: If you see someone struggling with sadness, anxiety, and negativity, listen to his story. You'll soon see he's living in a world where all he sees are things to blame because he lives without positive meanings for what's happened to him. The only cure is to restore the sense that there *is* a good reason for everything that happens.

Explain *That*, Why Don't You?

Years ago, if you'd said to me, "Everything happens for a reason," I'd have said that was a lot of bull. Things happened in my life that were so painful it's no wonder I'd had trouble finding their meaning, and I gave up looking. I now know that was a big mistake.

Lots of things happen to us that challenge our sense that everything happens for a reason. It can be anything. You get seriously ill at the worst possible moment. You think you've found the love of your life but something goes haywire between you and now the two of you are over. You've had one of those really painful childhoods. You screw up and lose a lot of money. Someone you love dies.

Yeah, we think, *maybe there's a meaning for some things that happen, but not for* this.

And even if we still have a shred of faith left that there is meaning in these events, we don't know how to find it. After all, the events in our lives don't come to us with labels attached telling us what they mean. We can spend years searching in vain. We ask friends, but they haven't gone through what we have. We ask someone who has gone through something similar, but that person is probably struggling to find meaning, too.

At some point we might be tempted to give up the search. That's what happened to me. It took one of my patients to wake me up and give me the hope that we can discover the meaning of the events in our lives. Everything important I've learned about how to do my job I've learned from my patients. Scott* was one of my best "teachers."

The Message in the Bottle

We all have dreams of what we'd like to do with our lives. When Scott first came to see me many years ago he was dreaming about going back to school and becoming a landscape designer. But he was afraid to give up his well-paying job. As you can imagine, addressing underlying issues of anxiety, low self-esteem, and identity played an important role in our work together. Soon, though, our work was all about helping him get what he needed to make his dream come true. He ultimately completed a two-year program at an excellent school and eventually opened his own little landscape-design business. He felt fulfilled.

---

* This book is filled with stories of real people, some from my research, some from groups I ran, some from patients. I promised complete privacy to everyone, the only way to ensure that they and everyone I talk to in the future would fully open up. So I've changed all names and identifying details. But I've honored the essence of everyone's story, the truth of their lives, and the core of what they have to teach us.

Several years later Scott came back to work with me. Sadly, he had non-Hodgkin's lymphoma, and he thought he was dying. (Scott's cancer eventually went into remission. He's still okay.) He said he wanted to discover why this terrible disease had happened to him just when his life was starting to work out. "Isn't this really a theological question?" I asked Scott. Truthfully, I didn't want to deal with a question like this. My attitude at that time was that you could never find an answer. And anyway, the most important thing is to make the best use of the time you have remaining. Why ask why?

But Scott, bless him, held onto his need. He was about to teach me an important lesson about how helping people is ultimately about helping them find meaning. After I'd dismissed his question Scott looked at me with tears in his eyes as if I'd betrayed him and said, "You don't understand. I don't want to die feeling like I was just some squirrel that got run over on the highway of life—hey, man, bad luck. I know that I'm *not* just a victim of a game of chance. I can't believe that I live in a universe where the things that happen to us don't have any meaning. There *is* some meaning in this, a message in a bottle for me. The message feels just out of reach, but it's very important to me. *Help me get that message.*"

Somehow *that* got through to me. I remembered how much I, too, had wanted to *get that message* back when I was a kid. (In a few moments I'll tell you about all the things that had happened to me and my family that left me hungry to find some kind of meaning and how discouraged I got when I didn't think I could find any.) Looking in Scott's eyes, I lost my sense of being pissed off at the universe because the things that happen to us don't come neatly labeled with their true meanings. Scott's need reawakened my own and all the hopes that came with it. I'd thought my need for meaning was dead. I'd acted as if it were dead. But the utter genuineness and *validity* of Scott's need made me realize that my own need for meaning had never died. Suddenly I felt a whole new connection to Scott, to my younger self, and to a world of people who were hungry to feel that what happens to them has meaning.

There was just one problem: How in the world could I help Scott discover why he'd gotten sick and might die if I couldn't help myself? I found myself terribly moved as I told him that I saw how this situation should have meaning and then confessed that I didn't know how to help him find that meaning. I felt I'd failed him. And I felt terrible about it. But I made a promise to myself that I would learn how to help people find the true meanings of the events in their lives.

Scott called several months later. He obviously wasn't as disappointed in me as I was in myself. I guess we all know how tough this search is. He had a note of triumph in his voice.

"I know why I got sick!" he said. "Look at where I was in my life. I'd made a lot of progress, but I was still frightened of so many things—flying, confrontations, bad news, you name it. Here's the gift getting sick gave me. Every day I'm learning not to be afraid, big-time. Death is the big confrontation. Once you face death, how can you be afraid of, like, someone rejecting you? You know, it's true: Cowards die a thousand deaths, heroes die but once. I'd rather live a short life without fear than the living death of a long life filled with fear.

"And I wouldn't have discovered any of this if I hadn't gotten sick. I don't know how much time I have left to live, but in the time I have left I'm feeling more alive and less afraid than I ever did before."

Everyone who survives something feels they have a new lease on life. But Scott felt he had a new lease on life even when he thought he was dying. Understanding that there was meaning in what was happening to him, discovering what that meaning was, made all the difference for him.

It made all the difference for me, too.

A Voyage of Discovery

———◆◆◆———

That was the beginning of my own voyage of discovery. *Wow, I thought, it really changes everything if you can discover the reason why some life event has overtaken you.* But I was still skeptical—I was far from convinced that Scott had discovered the real reason why he'd gotten sick or if a real reason could be discovered. But it had meaning for him, and as a therapist, I had to take this seriously. *Just imagine, I thought, if I could help other people discover what Scott was lucky enough to discover. . . .*

Deep down, of course, I knew how badly I needed this myself.

My Story

I'm sure I've had more than my share of blessings. I've been happily married for a long time. I have two great kids. I have good friends. Over the years it's been my privilege to help hundreds of thousands of people, and I love my work. So maybe you're wondering, "Hey, what does Mira know about what it's like to go through something really bad?" Good question.

I grew up with loss baked in my bones. As a child of Holocaust survivors, I lost the entire world in which I was supposed to grow up. Yeah, my parents survived. But everyone else in my family was killed: my mother's seven brothers and sisters, my father's five, all four of my grandparents.

I also lost the early years of my childhood. I was smuggled across Europe at the bottom of a hay wagon. I almost died of dysentery when I was three months old. I lived in a refugee camp for the first four years of my life. A barracks full of grown-ups recovering from shattered lives doesn't make for a good-time nursery school.

When I was four my life again turned upside down and inside out. I lost my father and my sister—my parents had gotten divorced and my father and my sister disappeared from my life. Then I left the only world I'd known, the refugee camp, to come to America.

When I arrived in New York I was so skinny that one of my distant relatives burst into tears when he saw me. My mother went to work in a clothing factory, and I had to take care of my brother. She eventually remarried, but my stepfather was no bargain. And we were poor—I didn't get a new dress until I was ten, and I bought it for myself with the money I'd earned baby-sitting.

Searching for Meaning

The parts of my childhood that were tough for me were not the parts that were touched by history. History is invisible to kids. The parts that hit me hardest were the ones that affect millions of Americans: seeing your parents break up, losing a father, not having money, feeling like an outsider, not having a happy family life.

Like everyone else, I grew up asking myself why all this had happened. I really wanted to know! I was afraid—if my past was meaningless, my future would be meaningless, too. But if I could discover why these things had happened to me—even better, if I could really feel that something positive had come out of them—then I could feel safe going forward.

I was very religious, so I did what lots of people do who are struggling to uncover the meaning of the events of their life: Every night I prayed to God to tell me the reason these things had happened to me and my family. When I got older I asked for some kind of explanation for the Holocaust itself. But if God was telling me, I didn't hear Him then.

You can only hit your head against a stone wall for so long. Eventually I grew tired of asking why. So I went the other way. I decided it was a stupid question. I had wanted an answer so I could feel stronger, but now I decided I'd be the kind of person who was so strong she didn't need to know why.

God Gets Called on the Carpet

But I never forgot that people's hunger for meaning was very real. I saw this when I was nineteen. My brother's wife had just given birth to their first child. The baby's arms were twisted into a tortured-looking position. He had trouble breathing. He couldn't nurse on his own because his sucking reflex was defective. The doctors knew that he almost certainly wouldn't survive, and if he did he would have to spend his entire life being completely cared for.

I spent those first days with my brother as the doctors examined his son and learned the full extent of his difficulties. Finally, when my brother couldn't take it anymore, he left the hospital and I went with him.

I'll never forget what happened when we reached the parking lot. My brother had been a tough street kid, a gang member, an MP in the army. Now he was crying. I'd never seen that before. What he said was "Why did this happen?" He wanted someone, the universe, God himself, to be called on the carpet and show that there was some meaning in what had happened to his son. But I didn't know how to find the answer for myself then—how could I help my brother?

About a year earlier I'd witnessed a situation in which God really *was* called on the carpet. It involved my sister-in-law's brother. Everyone thought of him as a once-in-a-generation wonder—brilliant, handsome, athletic, thoroughly good. The summer before he was to start college he was working as a counselor at a camp for kids with health problems. He was playing baseball, standing in the outfield. There were clouds but no threat of rain. A bolt of lightning came out of the sky and killed him instantly.

The odds of this happening must be one in a billion. Our shock and sense of loss were overwhelming. Why would this have happened to anyone, and why did this happen to him, of all people? As the weeks went on the question started to obsess everyone in our community. Eventually professors and clergy held a symposium in which they tried to pierce the veil and discover why God had let this happen.

But they couldn't come to a conclusion. You know how it is. People either say God is all-knowing and all-powerful, so who the heck can figure out why He does stuff, or they say God is one step removed from the day-to-day running of the universe, so why look to Him for answers.

There was my family and all those smart people, and millions like them, convinced that the search for meaning is necessary for our souls. And there I was—convinced there was no reason why things like this happen. They were right. I was wrong.

The Search Begins Again

I stayed stuck in my state of skepticism and error until Scott opened my eyes to the possibility that we can find positive meaning in anything that happens if we just know how to look for it. But at that point all I knew for sure was that *one* human being had discovered this.

Here's the thing, though: Even if I didn't know the secrets of the cosmos, I knew people. So I figured that if there was one Scott, there had to be a million Scotts out there who had discovered reasons for the events in their own lives while the rest of us were still searching.

I made a decision to look for these people and learn from them. Of course, this is how we always do research here at The Chestnut Hill Institute, so that part was nothing new. We look at some difficult task—parenting teenagers, keeping love alive, maintaining peak emotional energy, figuring out how to change your life—and then we search for men and women who have succeeded at this task so that everyone can learn from them.

And that's what I did here. I cast my net wide, broadcasting requests for people who'd found a meaning for a negative event in their life to come forth. I wound up talking to hundreds of people, and I asked all of them, "What reason did you eventually find? How did you find it? And what difference did it make to you?"

Seek and Ye Shall Find

It turns out there were lots of people who'd been where Scott and I had been, hungry for meaning but unable to find it. Like me, many of them had gone through a period where they'd given up hope. But like Scott, they kept looking . . . and looking . . . and looking. Eventually *they found the meaning of an event that they'd thought had no meaning.*

One guy discovered meaning in a friend's death when he said, "Okay, that house I was wanting to build with my own hands—no more delay, I'm doing it now." And so he built it and began the slow process of changing from being a guy who left all his dreams on the shelf to being a guy who understood the importance of making a dream come true every once in a while, even though there's never a convenient time for making a dream come true.

Sometimes it was the healing but oh-so-slow hands of time that brought people their discoveries. Sometimes it was an inner struggle, a dark night of the soul. Sometimes it was falling into the path of a wise teacher. Eventually, though, they found reasons that made sense to them and allowed them to move forward with inner strength, feeling confident and full of hope.

Still, I wanted to be careful. What good is discovering a reason why if it makes you miserable? So I also took a measure of how satisfied these people were with their lives. That helped me focus on the lessons and gifts that produced good outcomes like growth, happiness, and emotional energy.

By the end, I felt I'd struck gold. It turns out that people *can* find positive meanings in absolutely everything that happens to us in this crazy world.

What I learned about how everything happens for a reason changed the way I see life, myself—everything. It will change the way you see everything, too.

Ten Reasons, One Basic Principle

—◆—

As I talked to people about the reasons they'd found, at first I was dazzled by the variety. There were as many reasons why as there were people, and sometimes more, because a lot of people found more than one reason.

But sometimes life offers you a wonderful surprise by being a lot simpler than you'd thought. I looked for patterns in all the different reasons people had found. I used statistical analysis and seat-of-the-pants analysis. As I kept sorting, matching up one person's reason with another's and being delighted at all the connections I found, I saw that ultimately *there are only ten different meanings for the events in our lives.*

Inside the Mind of God

I sat there at my computer and typed out a final list of the ten different meanings I'd found. Then what I was looking at hit me. *Holy smoke,* I thought. If everything in our lives happens for a reason, *these are the reasons.*

If one person, like Scott, comes up with a reason, you can say he's just telling himself a story. But this was *it.* These were *all* the reasons there are. These are the lessons life teaches us. If the universe really is a nurturing place designed to help us grow, then this is what that nurturing is all about.

And then for a long, spine-chilling moment I looked at the ten reasons and felt I had a glimpse inside the mind of God. Not literally, of course. But as Dorothy Sayers says in her book *The Mind of the Maker,* just the way you can know the mind of a human creator through his words and works, you can gain a sense of the mind of the Divine Creator through His words and works.

I think that's true. Think of the best teacher you ever had. Your third-grade teacher, a college instructor, or someone who taught you crafts or swimming at summer camp. You knew that person cared, but it wasn't all fun and games, either. Great teachers often make you do an incredibly difficult task that seems pointless. *Why in the world am I having to go through this?* you ask. Then at some point, maybe years later, you discovered that the task had a wonderful meaning because it helped you learn something you couldn't have learned any other way. And then you finally understood what your teacher was doing. You had a view of what was going on inside your teacher's mind.

That's what I'm talking about when I say we just might be able to think of the ten reasons as giving us a glimpse into the workings of God's mind. Life itself sets us tasks, sometimes painful, sometimes unbelievably difficult. But suppose we get something valuable from these tasks. And suppose what we get is the reason we had to face these tasks in the first place. Then how can I not feel we're getting an insight into what God thinks we need to grow as individual human beings?

When we say everything happens for a reason, here are the reasons. You may not know which applies to you, but don't worry. You soon will.

The Ten Meanings of the Events in Our Lives

Everything happens to you for one or more of these ten reasons:

1. To help you feel at home in the world
2. To help you totally accept yourself
3. To show you that you can let go of fear
4. To bring you to the place where you can feel forgiveness
5. To help you uncover your true hidden talent
6. To give you what you need to find true love
7. To help you become stronger
8. To help you discover the play in life
9. To show you how to live with a sense of mission
10. To help you become a truly good person

This book is the story of these ten reasons, what they are and why they're important.

To Complete Your Journey

There you are, dealing with some event from your past or some situation in your present, thirsting for a way to find meaning in it. By answering a few easy diagnostic questions that will appear in each chapter, you'll discover which of the ten is the reason why you went through what you did. Of course you're not limited to just one reason! The more potential for growth you have, the more reasons you may find for what you went through.

Read the book through before you decide which reason is yours. Give the material a chance to work on you. You may be surprised by what rises to the top. By the end, you'll finally have the answer to the question *Why did this happen to me?* A hopeful, growth-filled future will be open to you.

Here's how to think of the ten reasons. Imagine that your life is a long, difficult journey. At some point you start running short of what you need. As you struggle on, you suddenly fall into a hole and hurt yourself. Ouch!

But it turns out that it's not all negative. On the contrary. If only you look, you'll find that right in that hole is something you've desperately needed to complete your journey successfully. And you wouldn't have found it if you hadn't fallen in that hole. As time goes on, you may even be able to say that the discovery was worth the fall.

A Warning

The reason something happened to you was to make something better in your future. The cosmos worked hard to give you this gift, so you damned well better use it. (Don't worry, I'll show you how.) If not, you'll just keep falling into holes until you can grasp the gift the cosmos keeps on trying to give you. So why not use it now, while you still have plenty of time?

One Basic Principle

Understanding the true meaning of the events in your life is more important than you might ever have imagined. How so? I discovered that there's one basic principle underlying the ten reasons:

> *The good that comes out of the bad things that happen to you is* to help you become your best, most authentic self.

Each of the ten reasons is a different way of helping you become your best self. And *your* reason is the specific resource you need to do a better job leading the life you were meant to lead as the person you were meant to be. Things happen to help you get rid of the parts of yourself that aren't you; to help you be more real and more yourself, not like everyone else; to help you lead a more authentic life; and ultimately to help you discover who you really are.

Circumstances often take us away from who we really are. And the further we drift, the more likely that it's going to take some final loss or difficulty to shove in our faces the fact that we don't even know who we are anymore. This helps us wake up so we can once again rediscover our true selves.

Laura had always thought of herself as a good person, loving, friendly, helpful. A single mom, Laura worked as a stockbroker. During a downturn in the economy she got laid off. The only job she could find in her field was with a disreputable, high-pressure outfit that aggressively sold low-priced stocks. Laura did this for many months, sinking lower and lower in her own eyes as she essentially cheated people out of their money. The pressure of her work forced her to become increasingly short-tempered with her daughter. One morning when her daughter spilled some milk as they were rushing to get out of the house, Laura hit her.

Laura was in a daze that day at work. As the afternoon stretched on Laura started crying. She came home and cried all evening. The next day she stayed home from work and cried nonstop.

At her most upset, she kept saying over and over, "Where is Laura? What happened to Laura?" The real Laura would never have hit her daughter. The real Laura would never have worked for a company like that.

Family and friends intervened. Laura got help and a good rest. Of course she never went back to that job. She reclaimed her true self.

Much more often, however, the process of self-discovery happens in a completely different way. Instead of starting out knowing who we are and then losing sight of our true selves, like Laura, we go along thinking we know who we are until some event comes along and makes us realize that we've *never* known who we really are, which then for the first time makes discovering our true selves possible.

Here's a story I heard from the archbishop of Canterbury, Rowan Williams.

Rabbi Yehuda was the holiest man of his age. One night he dreamed that he had died and was brought before the throne of heaven. The angel who stands before the throne said to him, "Who are you?"

"I am Rabbi Yehuda of Prague," he replied. "Tell me, my lord, if my name is written in the book of all who will share in the kingdom of heaven."

"Wait," said the angel. "I shall read the names of all who died today that are written in the book." And he read aloud the names, thousands of them. As the angel read, Rabbi Yehuda saw the spirits of all whose names had been called fly into heaven.

At last the angel finished reading, and Rabbi Yehuda's name had not been called. He wept bitterly.

The angel said, "But I *have* called your name."

Rabbi Yehuda said, "I did not hear it."

And the angel said, "In the book are written the names of all the people who have ever lived, for every soul is an inheritor of the kingdom of heaven. But many come here who have never heard their true names on the lips of man or angel. They have lived believing they know who they really are, but they don't know. And so when they're called to heaven by their names as who they really are, they don't recognize themselves. They don't realize that it's for them that the gates of heaven are opened. So they must wait until they know their true selves and so recognize their true names."

At this Rabbi Yehuda woke and, rising from his bed in tears, he lay prostrate on the ground and prayed, "Master of the Universe! Grant me once before I die to hear my own true name as who I really am."

Many more of us are like Rabbi Yehuda than we might think. On the surface we have complete identities—names, degrees, professions, affiliations. Then some cruel-seeming event comes along and wakes us to the fact that we've not known our true selves. At the same time it teaches us some lesson—one of the ten reasons for the events in our lives—that makes it possible for us to finally become who we really are.

Coming Upon Yourself in the Midst of Life

———————◆◆◆———————

Why in the world is it so hard for us to become the people we were meant to be? It should be easy. It was certainly no problem for my dog, Davy, and my cats, Tippy and Camille, to lead lives in which they were profoundly true to themselves. No authenticity problems there!

I think people today have trouble being who they really are because as social creatures we live in a hierarchical world in which we're highly dependent on others. So to get what we need we sometimes have to become less like the people we authentically are. We do this to gain approval, to pursue a livelihood, to hold a network of relationships intact. I can't tell you how many people told me that in order to survive in this world they have to wear a mask.

But you can only give so much of yourself away before you

lose yourself. This is why it's sometimes such a struggle for us to reconnect with our real selves. But then something bad happens that gives you just what you need to reconnect to your authentic self and life.

Many years ago, the poet Dana Gioia, currently chairman of the National Endowment for the Arts, lost his firstborn, who died of sudden infant death syndrome. He was only four months old. As Gioia put it, "Grief went through our lives like a wildfire."

You have to wonder how there could possibly be any redemptive meaning in the death of an infant. But it's precisely when it feels most impossible that there could be a reason that it's most important to find one. And, as you'll see, Gioia found it.

Of course, the reason may not justify what happened or give you back something of equal value. To be honest with you, I don't think a million meanings justify even one death. But this is not cosmic accounting. The meanings we get aren't intended to make up for what we've lost.

I don't think we're looking for full compensation anyway. It's not necessary. Whatever happened, happened. It's over. The loss is the loss. Now the question is whether there will be *any* gain, and that can only come by understanding the meaning of what happened. I think most of the time that if we can just find *some* good that's come out of what happened, we don't feel we need to try to balance the books.

But you need some reason so that out of the ashes of what happened you can say you found something you needed, not nothing. Once you find a personally compelling answer to the question "Why did this happen to me?" for the first time your attention is taken off the past that you can't control and focused on your future, which you have some control over.

This is what we're really looking for when we talk about closure. Nothing is ever really closed—not the kinds of things we're dealing with here. But there *can* be a total shift in where we place our emotional energy, from an unproductive focus on the past to a highly productive focus on the future. That's not closure, it's *opensure*. Whether or not we will make this shift is what's at stake here. If we do, a life of satisfaction, meaning, and joy awaits us.

That's what Gioia found. There was a period of mourning in which he wasn't able to think clearly. But then a light went on. He'd been a poet, but he'd always worked at a job to support himself. Now he decided to quit his job to focus exclusively on writing: no more doing anything but writing.

Why? Because the meaning of his son's death for him was that he needed to accept all the way down to the soles of his feet that he was a poet and writing poetry was what he needed to do with his time.

It was as if some dark force had said, "I will change your life in a terrible way," but then Gioia sifted through the ashes and found a gift—the opportunity to accept and serve who he really was and what was most important to him in life. Most of us don't listen to the universe unless it shouts at us. Gioia heard the shout and got the message. He woke up—and found himself.

Here's a second example. I took it from a *New York Observer* article dated January 27, 2003, about the journalist Oriana Fallaci and her bout with cancer.

When she started to recover, she began writing what she calls her "big novel." "It was 30 years that novel was sitting in my mind, and I haven't the guts to write it, because I knew it would be very long, very difficult, very complex," she said. "It scared me. When I got the cancer, I found the courage. I'm very grateful to the cancer, because it pushed me. I said, 'Hey, if you don't do it now, you die.' . . . So the dumb alien—I call the cancer 'alien'—must leave me alone until I have finished that book. If I died the day after I finish it, I die happy. Remember, if you hear that Fallaci died, but she finished the book— you must think Fallaci died happy."

For thirty years Fallaci put off realizing her dream because it terrified her. Her illness gave her the ability to let go of fear. She shows us how much better it is to feel that we live in a universe where the bad things that happen have benefits that can help us become who we were meant to be.

A third example has to do with a man named Thomas A. Dorsey. He went through hell, but it's clear that the meaning of what he went through was to help him find his voice and role in American music. He started out as a blues composer. He failed and went into a terrible depression. One day when he went to church he had a religious experience and he found God. But he still hadn't found himself.

Then, while giving birth to their first child, his wife died. The next day his child died. The day after that, more alone than ever and yet in a way closer to his true self, Dorsey wrote his great classic, "Reach Down to Me," which became one of Mahalia Jackson's signature songs. He'd discovered his voice. Dorsey was on his way to becoming the greatest American gospel music composer of the twentieth century.

None of us is any different from these three well-known people. Whatever reason you went through what you did, it was to help you get just what you've been needing in your life.

"You Mean It Really Is All About Me?"

When something happens in life to teach you a lesson, the lesson is all about you. Maybe this is one reason why it's been so hard for people to figure out the reason why something happened to them. They've looked too hard at the event and not hard enough at themselves.

I know—you'd think the meaning would come from the event itself. That's what everyone thinks. After all, that's what we're all doing, looking at some event and saying, "What does this mean?" But you can't read an event for its meaning the way you can read an X ray for a diagnosis. Events don't carry their own meanings.

We know this because people who've gone through the same event typically come away with very different meanings. Let me show you this by telling you about two women. Both were raped. Both were very deeply hurt. For a while they lost the ability to trust people, to trust life itself. And they were hungry to find a reason for why this could have happened to them. But each discovered a very different meaning, and in this lies an important lesson for all of us.

Let me tell you what they said to me. Here's the first woman:

Something good came out of that horrible experience. I'd always been treated like a nothing by boyfriends, friends, you name it. So I'd always thought I was nothing. Although I didn't realize it, that was the battle of my life—when was I going to wake up to the fact that I was someone who matters? I'll tell you—being raped really gives you the message that you're nothing. That was the horror of it for me. Being treated so powerfully like a nothing. Well, it took me a long time but I finally saw that if I think of myself as a nothing then I'm doing to myself just what that rapist did to me. And I refuse to do that. That terrible experience really forced me to accept myself as a worthwhile person. I promised myself I would never again reject the real me.

Now listen to what the other woman said:

It's funny what goes through your mind when something really terrible happens. When that guy was raping me I remember thinking, Well, you've spent your life being afraid, and being raped was one of your worst fears, and now it's happening. *And here's the part I'm ashamed to admit because what happened to me really was truly unspeakable. But being raped wasn't as bad as living with all the fears I had for all those years. That guy wanted me to be afraid. Why would I do that to myself? That was the beginning for me of learning to live without fear.*

There you have it: two similar events, but two very different meanings. This makes clear that the lessons you need to learn don't exist in the events themselves. They come to you *through* what happened to you, and they come because of what you were needing before that event even happened.

Welcome to Cosmic Kindergarten

Once I discovered the ten reasons for the events in our lives, I had to find a way to make sense of what I was holding in my hands. I trusted people—I knew that since these were the reasons people came up with, they were the real reasons. *But where did these reasons come from?*

My first step in making sense of this came when I finally figured something out. I'd been attached to the idea that the universe was a place of random accidents because I'd totally rejected what I'd thought was the only alternative: the idea of God as a puppet master, someone looming above us, controlling every little thing that happens, someone directly responsible for the car crash that killed your brother, your grandma's cancer, last week's plane crash, and the death of 6 million people in the Holocaust. I refused to believe that God could be this kind of puppet master.

I can't even imagine a God that would deliberately harm one hair on the head of one little baby. No cosmic plan could possibly be worth that. Ten thousand people don't die in an earthquake so I can wake up to the fact that life is something that needs to be savored! Or even so that everyone in the world can wake up to this fact.

How, then, *do* we make sense of the seemingly incontrovertible fact that everything happens for a reason?

Nature's Classroom

Whenever I'm confused, I turn to nature. It seems to ground me. When I think I understand how the natural world works, I feel I have a key to understanding how the cosmos works.

If anything about nature is true at all, it's that the natural world is a place of learning. Okay, maybe rocks don't learn. But plants and animals do. That's the whole point of everything we've learned about evolution. A species of living thing—a rose, a bee, a cactus, a camel—is a lesson learned in the face of a tough environment. It exists because some earlier species faced a challenge and "learned" in the sense of finding a new way to be. From the point of view of a gazelle, the reason why lions are fast is to make us gazelles faster. And the faster I get, the closer I get to my true gazelleness. If I'm a camel, deserts are hot and dry to give me my humps and in fact to give me a purpose in life, ugly creature that I am.

In nature, adapting or learning is the name of the game. Well, we humans are part of nature, but we have an extra added attraction. We don't need to become a new species to learn the lessons that are taught us by our tough environments.

If something happens to me, and if I learn from it, then I instantly become a new species of me. I've experienced a form of mini-evolution within myself. A lower form of me has evolved into a slightly higher form of me.

The Kindergarten Time of Life

In our human corner of the natural world, learning for us is also the name of the game. And since you and I have so much to learn, I think of human life as a kind of kindergarten. After all, it's in the kindergarten time of our lives that we get the sense in the deepest part of our being that everything happens for a reason. You fell down, so you learned to look where you were going. Your friend moved away and you learned that you could make new friends.

In most childhoods and in the happy part of all childhoods, life gleams with meaning and we all hope this will never stop.

Welcome to *Cosmic Kindergarten*. Shins are bruised, tears are shed, moods get blue. But this is the kind of kindergarten you never leave, nor do you ever really want to. Valuable lessons are always being learned and there are endless wonderful gifts waiting for us, especially as a result of the tough breaks we have to deal with. Maybe at your office the bastards really are out to get you. But the universe itself is a nicer neighborhood.

For people who are willing to learn, life is ultimately a nurturing place, and this learning gives meaning to our lives.

Here's an example. For challenging the old racist regime, Nelson Mandela, the first black president of South Africa, spent most of his adult life in prison. That's a big blow. After that you could easily spend the rest of your days filled with bitterness and regret.

But that's not how Mandela saw it. Sure, he condemned the political system that put him in prison. And he certainly would have preferred to have been free the whole time. But he saw his prison years as a tremendous opportunity. He was able to grow and learn. He found a voice, and he gained enormous stature in the fight for his cause. The world not only listened to him but revered him in a way that never would have happened otherwise.

Mandela understood in his bones that everything happens for a reason and he saw that the reason was so he could develop an inner wisdom he wouldn't have found otherwise. This became the foundation of everything he was to accomplish. If the steel of Mandela hadn't been hardened in the forge of prison, who knows if he would have been able to be so wise and effective when his time came to govern.

Cosmic Kindergarten sent Mandela to prison. It gave me a messed-up childhood. Who knows what it's had in store for you? In fact Cosmic Kindergarten works in thousands of ways, large and small, super subtle and incredibly obvious. It is quite simply *life*. But if we can view life as our own personally designed Cosmic Kindergarten, it gives us a reason to feel hopeful and much safer.

The Spiritual Side of Cosmic Kindergarten

———◆———

It very much helped me accept the idea that we live in Cosmic Kindergarten when I saw that this concept lay near the heart of spirituality in all its manifestations.

For example, there's a large movement in America today of people seeking spiritual understanding outside of organized religion. Spirituality today is a kaleidoscope of hopes and perceptions. But if there's any thread running through the incredible variety, it's a belief in a universe of connectedness, meaning, and hope.

Too often this belief is too vague to provide enough sustenance. But the idea of Cosmic Kindergarten nails it down. The things that happen to us get meaning from the specific ways they're connected to our personal growth. And so we're never lost—we're always in the process of becoming found.

And although they don't call it that, Cosmic Kindergarten is an insight reached by most great religions of the world. For all their differences, Hindus and Jews, Baptists and Buddhists, Methodists and Muslims, Catholics and Congregationalists all see the universe as designed to help you grow, to help you become more yourself and a better you, while at the same time getting more of what you need so your life works better.

Christians today don't subscribe so much to the old-fashioned idea of providence—that's the puppet-master view of God. What many Christians focus on is a view of the world as full of opportunities for grace. Something bad happens. God didn't make it happen, but there it is. And there we are, bruised and hurt. Then God's grace reaches out and makes some kind of healing happen. As Paul says in his letter to the Romans 8:28, "We know that in everything God works for good." Read any of Flannery O'Connor's wonderful stories to see this illustrated.

But grace usually goes beyond the fact that the pain eventually goes away. Grace in the best of circumstances takes the form of lessons or opportunities. And these are just the ones I've uncovered as the ten reasons why things happen to us. There you are, hurting, and God reaches out and gives you a free gift of Himself, a gift that helps you grow.

What's more, it helps you grow toward becoming more authentically who you really are, your best self. Here's how Archbishop of Canterbury Rowan Williams put it: "The act of creation can be seen as quite simply this—the vocation of things to be themselves. And to talk about God as your creator means to recognize at each moment that it is his desire for you to be the person you are. . . . The Holy Ghost calls us to be more, not less, ourselves—teaching Peter to be more Peter, John to be more John." And this call happens with particular power in the opportunities for grace offered by the tough things that happen to us.

What about Jews? Check out the Bible. In the Old Testament, God is many things but he is preeminently a teacher. Of course, he's sometimes a teacher who gets so mad and disgusted that he creates a flood for forty days and forty nights. But we've all had teachers in school who got easily frazzled. It doesn't mean they didn't want the best for us.

So here, for example, is God in Isaiah 57: "Because of their wicked covetousness I was angry; I struck them, I hid and was angry; but they kept turning back to their own ways, but I will *heal* them." Whether he's in an angry or a merciful mood, everything God does is for the sake of teaching us the lesson we're needing to learn. When he talks about how he'll "heal" us, we're to understand "teach and help us."

In fact, the entire Old Testament is organized around the concept of God teaching us through the events in our lives. Not only is God trying to teach, but the Bible is a teaching tool. *Rabbi* is just the word for teacher. God is a teacher, and history, our story, is the textbook.

There is a set of traditions that has had a huge influence on the spirituality of Americans today. I'm talking, of course, about the religious traditions of India, especially Hinduism and Buddhism.

For thousands of years, Hinduism has seen life as a classroom. Instead of saying you're born, you live, you die,

Hinduism says you're born, you learn, and you're reborn—this is the idea of *samsara*. Everything you do, think, and feel creates consequences, or *karma*. The soul learns from this and progresses, or fails to learn and is held back (like a poor learner in school!) until it learns. Of course, at the heart of the Hindu tradition is the guru, the person who turns darkness (*gu*) into light (*ru*). The guru, in other words, is a teacher.

Buddhism also emphasizes the lessons that are necessary for us as we encounter the events of this world. In fact, in Buddhism learning is key to what the soul needs to progress. All existence is bound by *pratityasamutpada*, the twelve-membered chain of causality. And the first link in this chain is ignorance. Ignorance starts the chain that binds the soul to the cycle of rebirth and suffering. Only when ignorance is overcome (through learning what the events in our lives have to teach us!) can we liberate ourselves from starting the cycle yet one more time and so finally achieve nirvana.

You may come from a religious tradition that's different from those I've mentioned. Think about how your tradition presents a view of life as a place of learning, mediated somehow through the hand of God.

What about me? How would I be able to accept the possibility that God was playing a direct role in Cosmic Kindergarten? Here's how I finally worked this out. I could accept that there was some Higher Power behind Cosmic Kindergarten if this were consistent with what I know about how nature works.

The fact that nature is knowable is a great gift to us. Ultimately it's a gift of freedom: We're free to understand and act in this world, to create new things, new possibilities. We're not utterly paralyzed the way we'd be by the unpredictability of an unknowable universe. Imagine if you dropped an apple and sometimes it fell down, sometimes up! You'd never be able to figure out how to make a rocket ship.

Nature is knowable because it operates via the rules of physics. You'd think these rules would exclude God's presence. Either God works within the rules and has no freedom, or God violates the rules of nature and ends our freedom, condemning us to live in an unpredictable world. So it would seem impossible to have both a world that's described by the laws of nature and also a world in which God is free to operate.

But here's what physicists have explained to me (and I appreciate their patience with someone as ignorant of physics as I am). It turns out that God does have freedom to operate in His rule-bound universe. The laws of physics don't cover everything. The universe contains infinite opportunities for random outcomes, and it's here that God has created his own opportunity to extend His teaching, healing hand.

Some of these opportunities for God's freedom exist at the subatomic level. Quantum theory has taught us that we can only know the probabilities of subatomic events. So, for example, we can never predict the exact position or direction of an electron, any more than we can predict what you'll get on one roll of the dice. Only God can determine what actually happens given the probabilities.

At the macro level, there are more opportunities for God's freedom. According to chaos theory, small initial changes can have indeterminate outcomes in large, complex systems like the flight of a butterfly or a cyclone or a supernova, just the way showing up for that event you'd planned to skip can result in your getting a tip that leads to a new job. Here too God has the freedom to extend His hand without breaking His own laws.

Bottom line: We have a rule-governed universe that is full of openings for God without His having to violate the very laws He created.

The universe still makes sense. We're still free to act. And God also is free to act. A Cosmic Kindergarten with God in it now makes sense.

A Look Ahead

Each of the next ten chapters discusses one of the ten possible meanings of the events in your life. Each points to ways Cosmic Kindergarten has custom tailored a learning experience just for you.

None of the ten reasons is more important than any other. And remember: There may be more than one reason to explain *your* life event. What matters is that you get what you need to become who you really are, your best self.

You'll hear the stories of people who've struggled with the same issues you have. But the most important story for you, of course, is your own. By the end, you'll have discovered the reasons for the events in your life.

part 2

The Ten Reasons

Squirrels in the Desert

———◆◆◆———

Feeling at home in the world is like feeling at home where you live. Suppose you've just moved into a new place. It's nice, but it feels a little cold and alien. Then you fix it up. You bring in furniture that looks and feels right to you. You arrange your furniture in a way that suits your lifestyle. You add in some of your old stuff and notice immediately how much more familiar everything looks. And then one day you feel at home there.

That's what feeling at home in the world is like, and it's much more important. The problem is that you can't rearrange the world to suit your taste. All you can do is find a place in the world that feels like home to you. This includes friends, the work you do, the kind of community you live in, ways to express your beliefs and creativity. When you find something like this, if you do, it feels wonderful.

Here's how some people have described it: "Everything in my life feels right to me now." "I feel I've come into my own." "I feel like myself for the first time." "I finally feel free." "I know what I want and I know I can get it." "I trust myself to take care of myself."

But it's not always easy to find a home in the world. Most of us have had experiences like this: You're in a new relationship. The other person certainly looks good on paper. And he or she is definitely a nice, friendly person. You should be great together. But it doesn't feel right. You're just not at home with this person.

It's the same when you don't feel at home in the world. Even if things look perfect, they're not perfect *for you.* Your life may look great, but you don't completely feel you belong there. This doesn't mean you feel like a weirdo. It doesn't mean you don't feel at home in *any* way. It's just that you're one of those people who hasn't yet found a life that feels completely right. In one way or another you don't feel as if you fit in. You may be good at hiding that feeling from everyone else. But it's hard to hide it from yourself.

And when you don't feel at home in the world, you imagine that there's some different career that would be right for you, some other person you could share your life with who would be right for you, some other place you could live that would be right for you. But you may not know what's missing and you may not know how to get it.

No issue is both more important and more subtle than feeling at home in the world. It's like being able to breathe. None of us turns cartwheels because we wake up able to breathe. We don't even notice it most of the time. But you'd sure notice it if you couldn't breathe. In the same way, some people only realize what it's like to feel at home in the world when they've lost it, when something happens to drag them out of what feels familiar and right to them.

When we don't feel at home in the world we need help, and Cosmic Kindergarten is designed to give us just the help we need, if only we pay attention. Often what we need to bring us home is a tidal wave. For many of us that tidal wave has already happened.

Tasting the Wine of Life

Let me share a wonderful letter I got from my beautiful friend Julie just after she died a while ago. I can still see those big, warm, brown eyes of hers looking at me so filled with hope, even near the end.

Julie was a painter. I'd wandered into a Newbury Street gallery one cold, rainy Saturday morning. The fresh, bright, warm, and mostly primary colors of her landscapes immediately grabbed me. I knew that someone who painted like that would be a person filled with light. Julie happened to be there that morning and we started talking. As I got to know her I found that she was as colorful and friendly as her paintings.

Sadly, Julie had a chronic kidney condition. A couple of years later, she developed end-stage kidney failure and died.

You might wonder if it's possible to see that everything happens for a reason *no matter what.* For example, can a person say everything happens for a reason and the reason *I'm dying* is ...?

That's what Julie's letter shows. In my experience, everyone who has time to get used to it finds a way to make sense of their own dying. And if you can find meaning in your own death, you can find meaning in anything.

My dearest friend Mira—

If you're reading these words, I want you to know I'm happy. Dead, but happy. LOL. I don't know if anyone who hasn't gone through what I've gone through can understand this. Sure, you don't want to get sick, and then when you find out you're sick you don't want to die. But at some point you get really sick and then you realize, Oh, death can be pretty damn useful. *It's a good thing, when the body wears out. I kind of think of death as my friend right now.*

I found peace a while ago. At first I really, really didn't want to die. But once I accepted the fact that I was going to die, I actually went through a pretty good period. The way I was feeling then was, Jeez, this sucks anyway, so why should I make it any worse than it has to be? *Really, why ever suffer more than you have to?*

That gave me a chance I think many of us never get: to look at my life and savor it, like when you sip wine at a wine tasting. All the living in the future is gone. You realize how much of life you've spent trying to get somewhere without taking the time to ever actually be *somewhere. Well, I wasn't getting anywhere anymore. This was it.*

Now here's the thing. This is what I want you to know. Hey, I'm reaching out from the grave to tell you this. (Kind of a creepy image, but how many times do you ever get to use it!) You know, I never felt I jibed with life all that well. I just didn't get what was going on a lot of the time. I always felt a little like a misfit.

Then I remembered back to that period when I'd cry and cry,

Oh, God, I don't want to die, why is this happening to me? *And then it hit me. I realized that that terrible regret I'd felt was really a wonderful gift. Wow. I was sad about saying good-bye to life—that's so great! It means my life was good. It means my life* was *home to me.*

It's such a paradox. In a way, my losing my life gave me the gift of seeing that I'd had a good life. I'd loved it and it had made me happy. My dying gave me my life.

Love forever,
Julie

Julie had been a huge inspiration to me for so long. Losing her was hard. But what a gift she gave me when she died! She validated my sense that many more of us struggle to find a way to feel at home in the world than we might guess. Julie showed me that a person can discover positive meaning in absolutely anything that happens. Julie found meaning in dying by seeing how it gave her a way to feel at home in the world.

Restless Souls and Other Special People

Here's how you can tell for sure if this applies to you. Answer the following diagnostic questions:

- Would you describe yourself as a restless soul?
- In high school did you have a hard time fitting in?
- Is there some secret, private part of you that you haven't felt comfortable showing anyone?
- When you see people who seem to really belong somewhere—people who live in a small town, or people

who come from a tight-knit family—do you envy them?

+ Have you felt that you've been looking for something in life for a long time but you're not quite sure what you're looking for?

If you answer *yes* to three or more of these questions, you can be confident that you went through what you did to help you feel more at home in the world. It was perhaps to help you understand why you chose the life you did. Or to show you a new and better way of living.

If this fits you, congratulations. This is a tough issue for many people. Behind lots of the smiling, confident faces you see every day, there's an unsatisfied yearning for a sense of at-homeness. But you've been given a gift designed to bring you home. You're that much more ahead of the game.

When you think about it, the idea that some huge event in your life helps you feel at home in the world is kind of strange. The life events that leave us hungry to discover their meanings are usually dislocations of some sort. They yank us out of our place in life and drag us into a new place where we don't want to be. So how can an event that catapults you into an unexpected path help you feel more at home in the world?

A tidal wave can bring you home when your previous home was a trap. There's a fine line between a home and a trap. Think about relationships. A great relationship can easily feel like the home for your heart. But what about a barely tolerable one, where convenience and inertia force you to try to overlook the dozens of ways you and your partner don't mesh? This is a trap.

Not because it's terrible, but because it's not terrible enough to push you into action.

Our life is filled with traps like this: the not-quite-good-enough job; the career you choose because it's secure and you're afraid the career you want is too risky; the apartment that's cheap and not where you want to live, but you stay because it's too good a deal to pass up.

Lots of times these traps are of our own making. We don't believe in ourselves. We don't know ourselves. It's as if we've glued ourselves into where we are and we need to use the glue precisely because the fit is so poor. Then it takes some dynamite to break up that kind of glue.

Maybe you've already lived through the explosion.

So That's What My Home Looks Like . . .

For some people, like Julie, the meaning of an event in their lives is that they are more at home in the world than they'd thought. Understanding why something happened to them means discovering a previously unsuspected at-homeness.

Here's another example. Zoe, twenty-two, was someone with a great but eclectic fashion sense who bought all her clothes at vintage clothing boutiques. She had short black hair and wore narrow black glasses and bright red lipstick. Think Cyndi Lauper meets Janeane Garofalo.

When Zoe was thirteen both of her parents were killed in a car crash. "I'll never be able to talk to anyone about what it was like to hear that both of my parents were dead—like you just can't breathe." Zoe was someone who had specifically come to me for help in discovering some meaning in her being orphaned. "I didn't have any brothers or sisters. But it wasn't just that I lost my parents. The other bad part was going to live with my grandmother. I know she did her best, but she didn't want me and she didn't have anything to give me. I've felt there are things you're supposed to get from your parents that I just didn't get: talking to them about stuff, asking them questions, learning how to do all kinds of things, like deal with other girls or boys—I needed that when I was thirteen. Some people think I still need it now! My mother was so beautiful. I wanted her to show me how to apply makeup and wear clothes. I needed my father to tell me I was beautiful. It's like I'm . . . *ill equipped*. That's how I feel, ill equipped.

"I just can't bear thinking something like this happens for no reason. I know there is a reason. I just don't know what it is, why I missed out on what I missed out on. I don't want to go through my life feeling I have all these missing pieces. It's like I'll never *come together*." All these words had spilled out of Zoe's mouth in a rapid, cool, even flow. Now she paused. "I'm starting graduate school in September, by the way. I'm studying black history. I'm going to be focusing on the slavery period, hopefully on slave narratives. There are so many missing pieces in these people's lives and in our understanding of their lives. I guess I have this fondness for things that have missing pieces."

"Let me ask you a question," I said. "Would you describe yourself as a restless soul?"

"I don't know," Zoe said. "I always feel like a misfit. Wherever I go it's like I'm looking at things through the wrong end of a telescope and I feel people are looking at me that way, too. Even studying black history . . . it's where I want to be and I love it. But I don't feel I'm on the same wavelength as everyone else. It's like I'm looking for something different from what they're seeing and I don't know what that is yet.

"So, I guess . . . yeah," Zoe said. "All that looking for something different—of course I'm a restless soul. I'm always thinking about doing something new or going in a different direction. No place I'm in ever feels quite right. It's like sitting in one of those chairs where you can never get comfortable and you keep shifting your position. That's how I think I feel in my life."

But I wondered if Zoe was more at home in the world than she thought she was. "What do you think your life would've been like if your parents hadn't died?"

"God, I used to romanticize that so much: how everything would've been perfect," Zoe said. Then she paused and sighed. "Look, they were really good parents. They really loved me. But they were also pretty conventional. And I was a wild kid. I had so much energy flying in all different directions. The image I have of my parents is that they were trying to contain my energy for my own good. I think that when I became a teenager I would've rebelled big time."

"Instead, since you were thirteen you've had to find your own way, but maybe you're less lost than you think. Maybe you feel the way you're supposed to feel when you're finding your own way. I'm saying you can find meaning in your parents dying when they did. It gave you an opportunity to find your own way sooner, with more freedom, to find your own home in the world in your own way. You're still searching, but the search itself is your home.

"And here's the thing. Your home in this world is special. You're not someone who can just get it off the rack. You needed all the time and freedom possible to get on with the business of finding it. Let me ask you this: You said you feel like a misfit; did you ever for a moment think that if you found your place it would be a cliché?"

"That was the one thing I knew," Zoe said. "That whatever my place ultimately was it wouldn't be a cliché."

"Your parents' death wasn't an empty catastrophe. You lost something huge. But you gained something that you needed in a special way. For a restless soul, you're remarkably well grounded. You're probably a lot more at home in the world than many people your age. You know you want to study black history. You know you want to focus on picking up the missing pieces in the lives of African-Americans and their heritage. You even have your own fashion sense."

Zoe glowed, like someone who'd just received two wonderful gifts. And she had. She'd seen that she was more at home in the world than she'd realized. She discovered that achieving this at-homeness gave meaning to her parents' death.

Zoe's story teaches us something very important about what it's like for some of us to feel at home in the world: Home isn't always what we think it will be. Some of us are restless souls. Some of us are oddballs—we haven't been formed by a cookie cutter. Restless, odd . . . so home for us might be hard to recognize, and it might be more of a process than a place, more of a road than a destination.

Make no mistake about one thing, though. Zoe found the meaning for what happened to her *in herself*, not in the event.

Not everyone who loses their parents at age thirteen is launched into searching for a way to feel at home in the world. But Zoe was. It wasn't her being orphaned but a restless, resistant, not-easy-to-pigeonhole quality in her that made her struggle to feel at home in the world. A terrible tragedy had meaning for Zoe because it gave her more freedom to resolve this struggle on her own terms.

That's Just Nuts!

Zoe was lucky. Lots of people haven't found their home yet. For them the meaning of what happened is to show them the way home. And this is something they need very much.

When you don't feel at home in the world, you feel there's something wrong with you, and the world doesn't feel right, either. Now here's the good news. You're fine. The world is fine, too. You're just a person in the wrong place. You're like a squirrel in the desert. Let me explain.

I've heard people call them tree rats, but I love squirrels. My big old house is built on land that slopes down toward the rear, and it's surrounded by tall trees. So my bedroom is four stories in the air, and I basically sleep with the squirrels in the trees. Every day I see them living their squirrel lives, playing, eating, running around, gathering nuts, and sometimes, in the middle of a warm summer afternoon, sprawling out on a branch dozing.

I can see every day that a squirrel's perfectly at home in a world of trees. But imagine taking that squirrel and plunking him down in the middle of the desert. This wonderful animal will suddenly feel depressed, anxious, confused, completely at a loss. There are plenty of animals who make a home in the desert, but not the squirrel.

There's nothing really wrong with that downcast squirrel in the desert. He's perfect. But he's only perfect when he's at home, in a place with lots of trees. In the desert a squirrel is an unhappy misfit.

Now imagine doing something stupid: taking that squirrel in the desert to a therapist so he'll feel better. As the squirrel himself might say, that's just nuts! You could do squirrel therapy forever but as long as the squirrel's in the desert, he's going to be miserable. But if you just pick him up and bring him to a place with trees, now he's at home and he's happy.

There are so many people who are miserable because they are squirrels in the desert. They think there's something wrong with them. They endlessly try to fix themselves but the fixing doesn't work. Yet they keep trying because it's hard to face the ways they're not at home in the world. And yet how simple it would be if they could see there's nothing wrong with who they are, there's just something wrong with *where* they are. Somehow, in some important way, their life doesn't feel like home to them.

But they can feel more at home than they ever imagined possible. They just have to look for ways that events in their lives are showing them the way home. Because this is what they need, this is something that the cosmos is trying very hard to give them.

Vicki was dating Peter, a rich, handsome Wall Street guy who used to play football for Yale. It was a fairy-tale romance.

They were famous in their circle for being the perfect, happy couple. One day Peter found out that on spring break of her sophomore year in college Vicki had gotten married. She'd been drunk. The guy had been a rock musician. The whole thing had been nuts. Vicki had bravely tried to make it work, but within weeks it was clear what a disaster it was. They got divorced. To Vicki this was one of those things that she didn't want to talk about because it never should have happened. It was just a hiccup in her life, a meaningless error of youth.

But Peter felt betrayed. To him this was huge. It wasn't like forgetting to mention a past boyfriend. This was marriage, for God's sake. He didn't buy Vicki's saying that this guy meant less to her than any of her old boyfriends. To Peter it was all about her withholding important information. He didn't know if he'd ever be able to trust her again. The fact that she was a wonderful person and they'd been incredibly happy together didn't help him forget and forgive. They broke up. Vicki was afraid she'd lost the love of her life.

Time brought a whole new perspective on this. Instead of feeling that losing Peter was an unmitigated disaster, Vicki started realizing that there was a reason why this had happened, a darned good reason. Here's how she put it: "Peter's dumping me eventually showed me what I need to feel at home in the world. Once I got over being heartbroken, I started to make things happen for myself. I did a lot of traveling, and I started writing about it and doing freelance publicity for travel destinations, hotels, resorts, things like that. And then I saw it so clearly. My destiny was *not* to become a housewife and socialite, which is where I was headed with Peter. I needed to have a life of accomplishment, action, and change. Peter was great, but he offered me a cocoon. I need to be an eagle."

Saved by the bell!

Free at Last

Suppose you're one of the people whose answers to the diagnostic questions showed that finding a home in the world is the meaning of some event in your life. But you don't know what that home is yet. How do you find it? As you'll see in a moment, the event whose meaning you've been trying to figure out will point the way home for you.

I'd like to ask you to do something. There you are, feeling somehow lost in life. Imagine that, feeling as lost as you do, you cross the deepest rivers and climb the highest mountains to find the cave where the wisest person in the world lives. "What can I do to feel more at home in the world?" you ask. This wise person shows you where to go next in your life by telling you the very story of the event whose meaning you've been trying to understand.

"That's it?" you say. "How does that point me in the right direction?"

"Think about your story in a new way," the wise person says. "You've been thinking of it as a loss. Now think of it as a liberation. What happened to you—it actually freed you up. And it didn't just free you up any old way. It freed you from some dead weight of the past so you could find a new home that would bring to life some part of you, maybe the best part of you."

This is exactly the conclusion that everyone came to who

found that the reason something happened to them was to show them the way home.

> It was always to free up some part of themselves that never would've come to light. Now they could burst free. And this part of themselves that was freed pointed directly toward where they would feel at home in the world.

Vicki had lost Peter and the life she would've had with him. But when she thought of this same story as a liberation, she immediately saw the direction it was pointing in, away from what would have been a boring, confining marriage, and toward a life in which she could make something of herself.

This freeing of the self so it can find its way home can be about anything. Maybe you'll realize that you'll feel much more at home in the world if you stop selling real estate and become a schoolteacher. Or it might be the other way around. Maybe it will point toward your getting out of your current relationship or finally committing to a relationship. It might involve being more committed to your art or to making more money. Whatever it is, it will have to do with living life more on your own terms.

Cosmic Kindergarten has given you the gift of liberation.

Look at what happened to you.

Find the way it freed you up.

Then you'll see an arrow pointing to the right home for you.

A Spiritual Homecoming

What happened to you might, for example, mean that you'll feel much more at home in the world if you open up the spiritual part of yourself. For some this means becoming more devout, more committed to some religious or spiritual practice. But for many others it could mean becoming more patient, more thoughtful, more in touch with what's really important to them in life.

One thing that's the same for everyone, though, is the fact that daily life as most of us lead it makes it hard to be spiritual. It's difficult to resist the crass and harried pressures of our workaday routine. No wonder it often takes the shock of a personal upheaval to liberate our spirituality. After a heart attack or a car crash it can be hard to return to business as usual.

As Carol put it, "I just went in for minor surgery. Recovering from the operation, I remember walking slowly down the hospital corridor thinking I was over the hard part when I suddenly felt so weak and tired. It was like my life essence was evaporating. I was convinced I was dying. It turned out that I'd developed a postsurgical clot. I really did almost die. When I finally recovered, my family was crying. They'd given me up for dead. *Why did that happen to me?* I wondered.

"Then I started thinking. After an experience like that do you just go back to worrying about whether the drapes match the rug? I couldn't. What happened to me freed me from all that. I'd been really religious as a kid, and now all I wanted was to get back to being the kind of person who cared about her religion. I've been so grateful that I had that brush with death.

"I wish I could say that I did something really amazing. But what I did was certainly amazing to me. It's not just that I went back to church. What's that? An hour every Sunday? No, I really made a full commitment to the church. I'd been away for so long I didn't know what that meant, but I just kept looking for ways to throw myself into it and then . . . well, I'd throw myself into it. I have to tell you that I kept wondering where this had been all my life. My life had been great but now I was really at home. I felt a sense of being myself that I hadn't felt since I was a child."

A Tale of Glory

It was no accident that Carol talked about *returning* to caring about God and her religion the way she had when she was a kid. Here's a valuable tip: If you really don't know where home is for you, then think of yourself as somehow having left home a long time ago. Home for you is that place you left. It's something from way back, maybe your childhood when we all have the most intense feelings about being at home. Whatever happened to you liberated you from something so you could go *back* home.

Here's another valuable tip for figuring out how what happened to you contains clues to how you can find your way home. Complete the following phrase: "There's something missing in my life that would make all the difference to my sense of being at home in the world and it is . . ." Okay, now think about what you just said is missing and think about how what happened to you gives you the chance to get it.

Here, too, I've found that people discovered again and again that they could only get what they needed to feel at home in the world by having gone through what they did. Think back, for example, to the great spiritual seekers and teachers in history. For most of them, their journey began when some calamity cast them into a dark night of the soul and liberated them so they could find what had been missing.

Take Brother Lawrence, author of the great spiritual classic *The Practice of the Presence of God*. His tale of woe was the only path to what turned into his tale of glory. This amounted to his feeling at home in the world in a way that perhaps few people ever have.

Born in 1614, Brother Lawrence became a soldier at eighteen, served in the Thirty Years' War, was captured, charged with being a spy, and almost hanged. He was released. Back in action, he witnessed many atrocities and was wounded in combat. After his military service, he became a servant, but he failed at this because he was so clumsy. Then he became a lay brother, the lowest rank on the religious ladder, in the Carmelite Order. He worked in the kitchen, but then when he developed painful gout he was forced to work in the loneliness of the shoe-repair shop.

He'd fallen as far as you can fall and he was all alone. But he was alone with God. And that, without his realizing it, was the home his life had finally liberated him to find. Alone with God at the bottom of the religious ladder, there was nothing for him to do but talk to God. It was there that he developed his amazing ability to live intimately in the presence of God through his constant conversations with God. The book he wrote about how to do this has been a classic for more than three hundred years.

Vicki, Carol, and Brother Lawrence were squirrels in the desert, perfect in their own way, but lost and troubled in another. Then, as happens in Cosmic Kindergarten, they went through some difficult events that liberated them in a way that brought them home to themselves.

The Confidence Game

There's another way to think about feeling at home in the world. It's about a deep kind of inner confidence: not *where* you are in the world but how you feel about being there.

Here's a story: If you're the son and grandson of admirals, and you go on to become a hotshot navy pilot, it's easy to be filled with a kind of cheap bravado about who you are and what you can do. You're the golden boy. You've got it made in the shade. That was the position Senator John McCain was in when as a young man he was shot down over North Vietnam.

He went on to spend five and a half years as a prisoner of war, two of them in solitary confinement. He was tortured. He suffered the further psychological torture of being offered early release because of his family position—but he knew that he couldn't accept that offer. What is the meaning of an ordeal like that for a person like McCain?

Life offered him a test he hadn't been bred to pass. And he made it through intact. He hung in there. He never did anything he was ashamed of. He survived. He helped his fellow prisoners. All this was a way for McCain to turn cheap bravado into the deep inner confidence that can only come from seeing what you yourself have been able to do.

McCain shows how an important part of feeling at home in the world is feeling deeply self-confident. What we see with him is what we see over and over again. We may go through a difficult time, but just by coping with those difficulties we develop a new level of confidence and trust in ourselves and as a result of *that* develop a much greater sense of feeling at home in the world.

This happens to a lot of people who don't even realize it. We miss it because we don't quite understand how confidence really works psychologically. It's not what you might think.

Suppose you're not confident that you'll be able to make a speech or host a dinner party. That means you suspect that what you bring to that activity won't be enough and the whole thing will be a disaster. So naturally you'll wish for what you don't have: an inner state where you'd feel utterly capable of being successful, knowing you'll deliver a great speech, or imagining you'll be complimented for being a great host.

But this isn't what it's actually like to be inside someone who is confident. Remember: Confidence only means something when you're talking about a task that's difficult. If the task is easy—something like making toast—you wouldn't even use the word *confident*. It would sound pretty weird to say, "I'm very confident I'm going to be able to toast this slice of bread." If the task is easy, you just do it without thinking about it.

Now here's what the inner world of confident people is *really* like as they face difficult tasks. They don't think, *I'm going to be successful.* They think, *I accept what I bring to this. I'm not going to be perfect. I might run into difficulties. But whatever happens I'll find a way to cope. I'll keep working at it until things turn out good enough. I'm not going to worry about things I have no control over. I'll be okay whatever happens.*

So when it comes to things that are difficult, confidence is all about feeling at home. Deep in the heart of confidence is a shrug, not a swagger.

Look, and Ye Shall See

Ultimately, Cosmic Kindergarten is just that—kindergarten. The gifts we receive are simple once we realize what we've got. The lessons that seem so hard when we were learning them seem so easy once we've figured it all out. At least that's how most people describe it afterward. If the meaning of what happened to you is that there's a way for you to feel more at home in the world but you're still not clear about exactly what that means for you, then I beg you, just look. Be patient. Keep looking. You have written the text with your life. If you read your life, you will understand the message the cosmos has been giving you throughout your life. If it's not clear at first, it will be if you keep looking.

Here are two people whose stories illustrate this.

My brother was a refugee kid, just like me, of course. He was eight when we arrived in America; I was four. It was tougher for him. Because he was older, it took him longer to learn English. He was a short, skinny kid who had to figure out how to survive in our tough neighborhood. Plus he was sick a lot.

What could he do? Develop a tough exterior. This worked, growing up on the mean streets of New York City. He joined the army, and when he came back he became an excellent craftsman and a good businessman.

But he still needed to find a way to feel at home in the world.

Then his first child was born sick and suffered and died. That was a terrible loss, but the universe is a place where everything happens for a reason. It took him a while, but he finally got to the point where he saw there was some redemption in his loss. Here's how he put it:

> You know when my son was born so badly messed up, I spent months going to the hospital before he died. In that special unit I saw all the other really sick babies, too, and their parents who were going through what I was going through. And I didn't really give a damn about them. My attitude was You've got your problems, I've got mine. But after my son died, it was just unbearable for me to think that my son's life and death had no meaning. Maybe it did have a meaning. Maybe he came here to teach me something. I didn't have any answers but I kept looking. Then one day this guy who worked for me was talking about his sister who had cancer and he said, "Why does she have to suffer like that?" Those were the identical words I'd used about my son! Somehow I realized that this guy was me. We were the same. There was no reason for me to think about him any different than the way I thought about myself. Suddenly everyone in the world felt like my brother. I don't know how else to explain it. I'd seen that everyone's just coming out of some trouble or about to go into some trouble. Every time you look into someone's face you're looking in the mirror.

So that's the meaning my brother finally found. It took something terrible to show it to him, but it liberated him from his tough, closed-off attitude and he saw that he was at home in the world in a way he'd never imagined. His sense that the world was filled with foreign faces jabbering in unknown tongues—which is how he'd seen the world as a child—was transformed into a sense that in the ways it mattered most, everyone was just like him.

My brother is seemingly very different from Cassandra, a young, carefree woman whose family had lots of money. She was traveling with friends through Central America, just looking for fun and adventure. She hooked up with the wrong people and the next thing she knew she was in jail on some trumped-up charge of antigovernment activity and inciting rebellion. Cassandra stayed there for months, not knowing if she'd ever get out.

Cassandra wasn't tough at all. She was spoiled, if anything, so of course she fought against the idea that there could be anything of value for her in being thrown into a Central American women's prison. But surprisingly quickly she saw what it all meant, like a lightbulb turning on. She's lucky, too, because she might never have seen it. Here's what she said:

> All those first weeks in that jail, everything was so disgusting, so scummy, and the guards were absolutely vicious and brutal to us. I kept thinking that things like this just don't happen to people like me. I don't belong here. These people belong here. But not me. One day I looked in the mirror. I was shocked at the hag I saw staring back at me. I was one of "these people." We were the same. That's when I dropped my attitude and started making friends and doing favors and finding ways to communicate with the other women. The people that I had thought were the scum of the earth became my sisters. Sometimes they literally gave me the shirt off their back. Now whenever I come in contact with people who get caught up in something terrible, I feel that they're me. The world is filled with my sisters. It's made me so much better a person.

Cassandra had grown up in a world of envy, competition, and social anxiety. The women in prison who'd seemed like alien creatures were the first people to make Cassandra feel she was part of a community, and that that community was her home. That this was even possible changed Cassandra's view of life. She vowed that when she got back she would never lose sight of this vision that you're at home in the world because you're connected to everyone in some way. I can't report that Cassandra went on to become an amazing humanitarian. But she did go on to become an artist's representative, and she brings a warmth and generosity to her work that makes her stand out.

There you have it: a tough guy, a spoiled young woman—two very different people, responding to very different events, coming from very different situations and backgrounds, using very different words. But they essentially got the same meaning from what happened to them because they both needed the same lesson. And they found it because they were looking for it.

If you'd known them before they went through their ordeals, you might've sensed they were cruisin' for a bruisin' and that life needed to teach them a lesson. You might've sensed what was missing in their development. Then something bad did happen and lo! Life sent them to school and gave them what they were missing: a way to feel at home in the world.

Three Gifts

———•◆•———

When you were born you were given three gifts.

One is the gift of life. You could breathe and feel and see and move and eventually think. Every day you're alive you celebrate this gift.

The second gift is the gift of *a* life. You were born somewhere, to certain parents. You were born male or female, American, Asian, or African. Your life had a setting, like a diamond has a setting. And every day, you live this specific life you were given.

The third gift is the gift of *you*. This is you as you really are, with all your warts and wonders. The point is that you are a gift yourself, all of you, not just the good parts but all the parts, and the ways all the parts add up to a whole.

This is important. You can't celebrate the gift of you and then disassemble it, sort it out into different piles, and then label one of those piles PARTS OF ME THAT ARE BAD. You celebrate the whole gift because every part of it goes into making you *you*. And who among us is so wise as to know which parts shouldn't be there? On the contrary. If everything has meaning, shouldn't we assume that even the parts we regret the most are somehow necessary to make the whole of you the gift it is?

Suppose someone gave you an entire island, with a house on it, and a boat to go to and from the island. Yet suppose the island wasn't quite literally paradise. Maybe it was too hot in the summer. Maybe there were lizards or mosquitoes. Maybe the house needed some work. Maybe the boat leaked. Would you accept this gift? Who wouldn't! You'd love it and accept it as a whole.

But lots of people have trouble accepting themselves. Let me tell you about a model who'd just starred on the runway of a major fashion show. There were other models there, of course, but somehow this was her magic night. She gleamed with an inner light. All the men wanted her, all the women wanted to be her. I'm sure everyone thought she had it made.

I saw her the following day. "At the end of the show," she said, "I was standing on the sidewalk with all these people telling me how wonderful I was, and then I turned the corner to go home and I was absolutely alone. I had no one to walk with me."

It turned out that she was ashamed of herself, her life, everything. Her boyfriend had just dumped her. With her constant travels she had few friends she could reach out to. She struggled with alcoholism. She thought she was fat. She hated herself. For an entire hour she sobbed, telling me these things.

This story is the rule, not the exception. Think of the most successful person you know, someone you think has totally got it made: maybe someone famous, maybe someone in your neighborhood. I promise you that if you got to know that person deep down, you would find ways in which he or she is ashamed of him- or herself. You'd find shocking stories of humiliation and surprising pockets of self-hatred.

There are millions and millions of men and women who struggle with self-acceptance and never attain it. It's very sad. But every once in a while something big happens to wake them up. It gives them a chance to see that they need to accept themselves, and it shows them a way to do it. Wouldn't it be helpful if something could happen in our own lives that would miraculously give us the gift of self-acceptance?

Maybe it already has. You're about to find out.

What She Got for What She Lost

Sarah came to me because she had lost her leg as a result of a car accident. The driver of the car next to her on the highway had lost control and veered into Sarah's car, which crashed through the guardrail and rolled over down an embankment. I was part of her rehab team.

At one point I asked her, "Has it been hard for you to accept yourself as someone with a missing leg?" If there was anything else missing in her life, I didn't know yet.

She was acting brave. "You know, when you lose two legs you

have to use a wheelchair. So I'm lucky. I have to hop around when I'm not wearing my prosthesis, but at least with it on I can still play soccer."

"Come on," I said. "Everyone who's lost anything pretty soon develops smart answers that help her avoid dealing with her loss. And that's good—you don't want to be vulnerable all the time. But I know you're not here because you're fine with having lost your leg."

Her face quickly took on the flat quality of someone about to cry. "Okay, here's what happened. When the doctors told me my leg was going to have to come off, everything happened so quickly I didn't have time to think much about it. I was just worried about dying. And right after the operation, the first couple of days, I kind of felt a surge of energy. I just thought, *Okay, fine, I'll deal with this, no problem*. But that easy period didn't last very long. You can only take 'perky' so far. Since that first week, it's been very hard, and it hasn't gotten easier with time. Little things are hard, everywhere I turn, standing at the counter at McDonald's—you name it. And I can't get used to people staring at me.

"Does losing my leg mean I'm going to be alone for the rest of my life?" Sarah asked me. "Even if I have a great prosthesis, when do you tell someone you're dating that you're really a one-legged gal? So how *can* I accept this when everything I'd expected in life is changed now?"

I suspected that having trouble accepting herself might go deeper for Sarah. If self-acceptance was an important issue, maybe the reason this happened was to finally make possible the self-acceptance she'd longed for.

Sarah answered the following diagnostic questions. Answer them for yourself:

- Would you say that you've lived your life overly concerned with what other people want and what they think is important?
- Does it seem like you're always trying to change things about yourself without making much long-term progress?
- Are you afraid to tell people close to you what you want?
- Do you often feel like someone who doesn't matter, or do you often let people treat you like someone who doesn't matter?
- Do you feel that if people knew the real you, they wouldn't like you?
- Do you have a clear dream of something you want to do or a way you want to live, based on what's most important to you, that you're not doing anything to make come true?

Maybe you were dumped by your college sweetheart, or spent too much of your childhood sick with asthma, or are not as good-looking as you would like to be. Whatever your life event is, if you answered *yes* to four or more of these questions, then what happened was to give you what you need so you can achieve the total self-acceptance you've been looking for.

Sarah went five for six. (You'll see how this applies to you in a moment.) We started in talking about the first question. She said, "God, I always focus in on what other people want, like what I want is stupid. When I woke up from the accident in the hospital, it was like this unusual situation. The doctors gave me these choices and I couldn't decide anything without asking every single person I knew what they wanted me to do.

"Even when it came to removing my leg—it was like it sort of had to be done, but the doctor wanted me to feel I had a choice except I didn't really have a choice. I could see in my boyfriend's face his feelings about living with a one-legged woman. So I kept asking the doctor about maybe not removing my leg. Of course, they can't be totally certain about everything. And so because they couldn't absolutely promise that it absolutely had to go, I was worried about how my boyfriend felt. And then when I did agree to the operation, the reason I did was that I didn't want to disappoint the doctor. When I woke up without my leg it was like I hadn't even chosen it."

"Is that a pattern you see in your life?" I asked gently.

"Oh, yeah," she said. "Like why did I become an accountant? Yeah, I was smart and good with numbers, but growing up I was kind of nerdy and I think my parents just figured that being an accountant would be a good safe profession for me to hide out in. And I completely went along with it.

"You know one of those other questions you asked me, *If people knew the real you, would they like you?* Well, I always felt, *No, no way.* I'm just this boring little person; I'm good at math, but I'm not all that smart or creative. I'm just, you know, a zero. I never got asked out a lot. Why would other people like me if I didn't like myself? And so, of course, I didn't have a right to go around saying what I wanted about stuff."

Self-Acceptance Is Just Around the Corner

Sarah was now in a position to discover that she'd been given a gift along with her loss. Losing her leg had plucked her out of the path she'd been on and had placed her on a new path where she would find the kind of self-acceptance we all long for. But how did this happen?

Everyone achieves self-acceptance the same way. It's like remembering someone's name. It's on the tip of your tongue. You've almost got it. You have a sense that because you want to remember it, you will remember it. But there's nothing, nothing, nothing, and suddenly there it is.

It's the same with self-acceptance. When you really get it, you get all of it, and you get it in a flash. And what you get is a kind of sweeping power finally to let yourself alone.

How does some big event in our lives bring this about for us?

There's something massive and mindless about a terrible event. Whether it's an attack, an illness, or getting hurt by tough economic times, the tidal wave that sweeps over us can make us feel like we're nothing.

It's the opportunity to shout back, "I'm worthwhile!" when life says, "You're nothing," that makes it possible for some people to gain that flash of self-acceptance and so find meaning in what happened.

Let's start with someone who's had trouble accepting him- or herself—maybe you, for example. You've probably been really hard on yourself. Maybe you've hung around in situations that aren't good for you, but you've stayed because, well, you're not sure you deserve better. Then life comes along and smacks you in the face with some disaster or difficulty.

Getting What You Deserve

What happens next doesn't happen right away and it doesn't happen to everyone. But it eventually happens to more people than you might think. You get fed up. You say, *Wait a minute, holy cow, I don't deserve this crap.* It hits you that you don't deserve to be treated this way by life. And then something else hits you—you realize that you've been treating yourself the same way.

> *If it sucks the way life's treated you, it's totally nuts that you'd be treating yourself the same way.*

That's it, then. For most people it's like a light going on. Self-acceptance was impossible, and then suddenly it's absolutely necessary and easy. What does this feel like? It feels like looking at the parts of yourself you'd hated or rejected but now you look at them and suddenly you feel they're okay. You can live with them. Maybe you even like them. For the first time in your life you appreciate the gift of *you* that you were given.

This is what I wanted Sarah to experience. "We know," I said, "that finding self-acceptance is the meaning of what happened to you, based on your answers to the diagnostic questions. But I think we can go beyond knowing *that* you went through what you did so you can achieve self-acceptance. Let's talk about *how* you will achieve it."

I asked Sarah to talk about parts of herself she'd had trouble accepting before she lost her leg.

"You know, the whole time I was growing up, my parents urged me to get married and have kids, although why they urged me to do something that's kind of natural for most people to do, I don't know. When my mom talked to me about being an accountant, the first thing she said was that it was good because I could do it part-time when my kids were little.

"But you know what I really wanted to do? I wanted to become a doctor. And somehow the way I was brought up or something made that seem really selfish. Then when I got hurt—I think this happens a lot—you see what the doctors can do for you and you feel so grateful, you want to be able to do the same thing for others. Then again I told myself, *Nah, you can't become a doctor.* I don't know—like I'd be inconveniencing people if I stood up and said I want to do that."

"But it sounds like that's your heart's desire," I said. "And you've spent your life rejecting it. Unless you accept it, you're not accepting yourself. If you were being accepted into a new group of people, like into a new church, how would you want to be accepted? With open arms. Well, that's how you have to accept this part of yourself. Open your arms to your own desires. Maybe a further reason why you lost your leg was to kind of slow you down so you could accept the reality of your wanting to become a doctor, while you're still young enough to make it happen."

"It's so funny that we're talking about this now," Sarah said. "When I first learned I was going to lose my leg, even while I was crying that no one was going to want me and I was going to be alone for the rest of my life, part of me had this crazy thought, *Now I can become a doctor.* That's what kept coming into my head. There are probably lots of one-legged doctors in the world. I think I'd always been scared to accept the responsibility for what I really wanted. I mean, that's taking on a lot. But I don't have to be scared of anything now. *So why not figure out a way to go to medical school?* I said to myself.

"What happened to me is almost like a metaphor. *Life played a dirty trick on me when it cut off my leg. So why would I cut off part of myself?* And that's what I'd be doing if I didn't fully accept my heart's desire."

Even the Smallest Event . . .

This is more or less what everyone I talked to said: "I accept myself because I see that I can't do to myself what life did to me."

Remember the two rape victims I talked about in a previous chapter? Forgive me for repeating what one of them said: "I'll tell you—being raped really gives you the message that you're nothing. . . . Well, it took me a long time but I finally saw that if I think of myself as nothing then I'm doing to myself just what that rapist did to me. And I refuse to do that. That terrible experience really forced me to accept myself as a worthwhile person. I promised myself I would never again reject the real me." That's how the light went on for her.

Even small events can wake us up to the self-acceptance we've been needing. Jack's story shows this:

About ten years ago I was on vacation with some buddies in New York. We were busy doing stupid stuff, strip clubs, bars, and so on, and on the third day I got up early to go out and buy a present for my mother. When I got back to the hotel all the guys had taken off! The only message they left was "Got tired of waiting. We decided to go to Atlantic City. We'll see you when we see you." I couldn't believe it. It was the worst insult of my life. I really felt hurt, and I hadn't been feeling so good about myself to begin with. Buddies don't do that to each other, so who was I that they would do that to me? I moped around for a while. Then I got fed up with moping around and just thought, Screw it, I'm in New York, I'm going to have a good time. *Since I was alone I started to think about what I really wanted to do. The next thing you know I'm going to the Museum of Natural History, the Metropolitan Museum of Art, a concert—stuff I would never have thought of doing when I was with those guys. I remember at one point thinking that everything happens for a reason. And I was glad for what had happened. It taught me that I could be . . . that I had to be who I was, and that meant most of all doing what I wanted.*

That's it, exactly. Jack's friends rejected him. He wouldn't reject himself. His friends abandoned him. He wouldn't abandon himself.

Here's another story that shows how even a relatively common event in our lives can give us a flash of insight that makes self-acceptance possible. Teri had caught the flu. It was a bad case and it lingered for weeks. Before she got sick she'd lived the kind of social life that was very important to her husband and that had been important to her parents: always throwing parties and going to other people's parties, going on vacations with other couples. She hated doing these things but she couldn't accept the part of herself that hated doing them. She felt there was something wrong with her for not always wanting to be with people, for preferring solitude.

As she recovered she asked herself, *Why did I have to go through this ordeal?* Realizing that her life was precious, Teri saw that she had to stop destroying herself the way her illness had tried to destroy her. And when she didn't accept herself and how she wanted to live, she was destroying herself. All this for her was the reason why she got sick.

So why shouldn't self-acceptance be just around the corner for you, too?

Picking Up the Self-Acceptance Habit

When we don't accept ourselves, we look at some bit of our bodies, our minds, our desires and we get worked up over how yucky it is. We're like a movie critic who's all excited at how much he or she hates a certain movie. If this habit weren't so destructive, it would be almost delicious, the way it's sometimes delicious to get together with a friend and talk about what a crappy person someone else is. We're using our energy and intelligence to reject ourselves.

The new habit develops as we use our energy and intelligence to accept ourselves. You've already seen that you can't and won't do to yourself what your life has done to you. So you've got the basis for self-acceptance. Now really throw yourself into it.

Accept yourself for having trouble accepting yourself. And why not? Life today is set up to make it hard for people to accept their weaknesses and imperfections. Just pick up any magazine, for example. Magazines are filled with articles showing you how to do things the right way. They're filled with tips on how to improve yourself. They're filled with images and stories of people who are better looking, more capable, and more successful than we'll ever be.

It's hard to come away from things like this thinking, *I'm fine just the way I am.*

Part of the problem comes from how much we want to fit in somewhere. It goes back to when you were in high school. Back then most of us were made uncomfortable by whatever made us different from everyone else. We just wanted to be popular. That's why most high school kids dress and talk just like the kids in their group.

Maybe the impulse to fit in is nature's way of helping us become team players, because that's how so much gets done in the adult world. So if you're fat, you learn to hate it because it's the kind of thing that gets you off the team. If you don't talk the way other people talk, they might think you're weird and shun you. If you're interested in something other people aren't interested in, you learn it's something shameful, something to hide.

So we all become hall monitors of the self. We scrutinize and criticize ourselves. And by hating or ignoring what's special about ourselves, we can't accept ourselves and so we throw away that all-important third gift we got when we were born: the gift of ourselves as we really are.

Of course, this is a much bigger issue for some people than for others. Some people have an easy time accepting most things about themselves; some people have a very difficult time. Why would this be especially hard for some of us?

Maybe we got a lot of criticism growing up. Maybe loneliness made us desperate to fit in. Maybe we just weren't wonderful enough in the ways we wanted to be wonderful. And maybe we looked at what was special about us and freaked out—it felt too gross or weird: like being gay in high school, like being a woman who always wants to be in charge, like being a guy who likes to daydream, like being a woman who likes to be alone. As a result many of us live like spies in an enemy land, vigilant against ourselves in case we might be found out.

Of course, plenty of us get the message that we are bad for being who we uniquely are. What's scary is how easily we swallow this message when it's offered in the guise of help. Let's talk about women for a moment, although the same kind of thing is true for men. Our society has an image of the Standard Woman. She's thin, attractive, well groomed, well dressed, and she smiles a lot. She may have a career but she still likes girly things: babies, shoes, cooking, interior decorating. She's nice and has lots of nice girlfriends. She works but she does the kind of work women do.

Now suppose you're a mother. You know a dark truth—that you yourself aren't as much of a Standard Woman as people think you are. Most of us inside don't live up to society's models. And you know this has hurt you. Either you've had to reject the parts of yourself that are different, or you've had to suffer at the hands of others for being different.

So you look at your daughter all ready to celebrate what makes her special and you get scared. You know how much easier her life will be if she's more like the Standard Woman. You know how hard her life can be if she doesn't fit the mold.

So as a good mother, you turn the vise. Turn, turn, squeeze, squeeze. The pressure's always on because you want your daughter to have a good life just the way your mother did with you—different issues, maybe, but the same pressure. Well, she may rebel, but she loves you and respects you and wants to please you. And so like many daughters throughout history, she ultimately agrees to dislike about herself the things she thinks you dislike about her.

Many of us have been treated this way. In the end, family, school, the workplace, and society as a whole can easily combine to give us this message: We want you to dislike about yourself everything we dislike about you, and that includes everything we think is outside the norm.

So she hates herself for being overweight, just as she was taught. Or she hates herself for not being interested in having kids to the point of denying to herself that she's not interested, just as she was taught. Or she hates herself for being ambitious, and so develops a thousand energy-consuming devices for pretending she's not ambitious, just as she was taught.

There it is, then, more than ample justification for understanding what a big job self-acceptance really is—until life comes along, kicks you in the pants, and makes it a lot easier for you.

Fat, Skinny, Tall, Short

Let's face it, when we talk about self-acceptance, we're really talking about liking ourselves. So I'll let you in on a deep, dark secret: Sometimes we fail at liking ourselves because we go about it in the wrong way. We think it's about having some big crush on yourself because that's what we experience when we really like someone else.

But that's not what it's like for people who really like

themselves. It can't be. We know ourselves too well to have a crush on ourselves. If you want to like yourself, accept yourself as you are. For most people that's all "liking yourself" really means. You see who you are, you let in the idea that you have good qualities, and you stop giving yourself such a hard time about your bad qualities. Isn't this what we do with our friends? We just accept them. Why wouldn't we do this with ourselves?

Then as you go through the pieces of who you are that you've had trouble accepting, it helps to remember that here, too, everything happens for a reason. Maybe you've had trouble accepting something about the way you look. How can you like yourself if you're fat, skinny, tall, short, or homely?

But there was a reason for that, too, maybe the same reason we've been talking about here—to help you accept yourself. In Cosmic Kindergarten everything that happens is in some way a gift or an opportunity.

Let's say you've struggled with being overweight. Sure, lose some pounds if you want to, but also know that you carry around a physical reminder of your need for self-acceptance. Every time you look at yourself you have an opportunity to say, "For me to like myself I have to like all of myself."

We can accept our flaws when we see them as vehicles for something that wouldn't have happened otherwise. Maybe there was a prideful element in your personality, and so being overweight is a way of keeping you humble. Maybe there was a perfectionist part of you, and a few extra pounds are a way of forcing you to remember that everything doesn't have to be perfect. "Oh, *that's* why I have a big ass," one woman said when I told her this.

Here's the discipline. Find your way to liking yourself by looking at what you've had trouble accepting and asking yourself, "How is this good?" And search for an answer, as if the wisest guru on the planet had given you this as the theme for your meditation. You've not found the answer yet because you've never asked the question.

Try Not to Try

Ultimately, self-acceptance is a matter of *seeing*. You see that by not accepting yourself you're doing to yourself what was done to you. Then you look for more ways to accept yourself. The one thing you don't do is "try" to accept yourself. It won't work. And you don't need it.

Everyone who works at helping people change understands that trying is not the solution. People try all the time and fail: like trying to lose weight, trying to keep your desk clear, trying to tolerate people who annoy you. You try, you hold on by your fingertips for a little while, and then it all falls apart.

And yet people succeed all the time *without* trying. I know one woman who kept trying to diet but never really made the changes necessary for dieting to work. The scale just told her numbers. The mirror just showed her images she was used to seeing. But then one summer day walking down the street she caught a glimpse of herself reflected in a darkened store window. She was horrified by this completely unprepared for glimpse of herself. Finally she *saw*. That gave her all the motivation she needed.

Here's another example of someone who changed because

he saw. This was a guy who smoked. All his friends and family had been trying to get him to stop for years. He kept trying. Nothing worked. Then his cousin, a lovely young woman in the prime of life, died after a long illness. The whole family was there. About an hour after she died he went to say goodbye to her. He bent over to kiss her on the forehead. It wasn't just that her skin was cold. It had a sensation he'd never experienced before. He felt death. And with that he saw what he needed to see to be able to stop smoking. He never smoked again.

That's all any of us needs. Over the years I've tried to put my finger on what pushes people over the line toward making real change. The best answer I've found is that it is this *seeing*. We see all the time, but suddenly we see something new and different that pierces us to the core. It feels as dramatic as the difference between the darkness of sleep and the light of awakening.

It's just that we also need something to make us see. And that's why the bad things that happen to us have the power to produce real change in the area of self-acceptance and in every other. Nothing wakes you up and makes you see like an explosion.

Practice Makes Perfect

It's a funny thing about the lessons we learn in life. No matter how much it costs us to learn them, no matter how deeply they're etched in our hearts, sometimes we forget them anyway. We need a way to put them into practice when we've forgotten a little of what we've learned. So in this case, how do we remember to accept ourselves when we start sliding back into old patterns?

If change happens when you see something big and new and meaningful, the key to maintaining that change is continuing to see. So we have to see when we're sliding back into old patterns. This requires vigilance. Too often self-rejection comes in the guise of "constructive criticism" or "a much needed kick in the ass." But if you can see that you're getting on your case for stuff you know has been very hard for you to change, then this is just self-rejection. See it for what it is.

A simple way to get rid of self-rejection is to ask, "Is this helpful?" Be honest. You've just said, "God, I'm so fat." Okay, so tell me: Does that help? I can't imagine it does. So get in the habit of answering back to yourself, "That's not helpful," every time you say something self-rejecting.

Another way to put an end to self-rejection is ask yourself whether what you're telling yourself is what a friend would say, or what an enemy would. Friends are supportive. Enemies put us down and undermine our confidence. So if you say something that an enemy would say, stop. Answer back, "I'm going to be supportive of myself. As a friend, what I have to say to myself is . . ." Then say something supportive.

Another good way to maintain self-acceptance is to remind yourself, "I'm not Superman. All I can do is try my best." When people struggle with self-acceptance, I've noticed that they judge themselves from too many angles. If you're a new mom, for example, that's tough enough all by itself. It can be hard to accept that you're a plenty-good-enough mom. But to think that you'll be able to look like a million bucks at the same time is just not fair. Most of us can barely do one thing well in life. And to do that one thing well, we have to let most other things go.

Finally, if you've been getting down on yourself, maybe this thing you're struggling with just isn't you. You want it to be you, but it isn't. Maybe you've come up with some great idea for a piece you want to write for your local newspaper. But then when you sit alone you can't bring yourself to put words down on paper. So why torture yourself? Maybe it's *you* to have good ideas, but it's *not* you to sit alone in a room for hours at a time and produce something out of nothing. Remember, self-acceptance begins and ends with being able to say, "*This* is who I really am, and it's okay."

And what's made all this growth into self-acceptance possible for you is that something happened in your life, and the meaning of what happened was so you could look at it and say, "I'm not going to do to myself what was done to me."

Smooth Sailing over Troubled Seas

———◆•◆•◆———

The journey of life takes place over troubled seas. Life is full of things that scare the crap out of us. Some fears are perfectly reasonable, but some are terribly damaging—they lock us in their grip, preventing us from embracing an important part of life.

Then we go through some painful experience and realize the reason we went through it was to give us a way to live without fear.

Sometimes the lesson hits us between the eyes. One guy was in a near-fatal car crash. He was told that there'd been a moment when his heart had stopped and he'd been quite literally brought back to life. He'd always been afraid of being poor, so he'd saved every penny. But having faced death and survived, he didn't ever again want to let his life be ruled by his fear of not having money. Now it was his time to embrace life.

Sometimes we're shown a way to live without fear without even realizing it. I'm thinking about a friend of mine, Mary, who also went through a wrestling match with death. A boat she was sailing solo down the east coast from Nova Scotia was caught in a horrible gale. For a day and a night she watched the sails get torn to shreds, the waves pound her mast into matchsticks. The cold sapped her energy. Every minute she expected to die.

But somehow the boat held together and she made it through. As she staggered onto shore, a resolution suddenly crystallized. She'd always hated being a lawyer, so she decided to quit her job.

Was leaving the law the reason that Mary went through that ordeal? Only on the surface. Mary quit because that ordeal gave her something that made it possible for her to quit—a way to let go of a deep and powerful fear.

People thought Mary was a daredevil. Sailing alone on wintry seas, Alpine skiing down the toughest trails, or scuba diving at extreme depths, she seemed the very model of a woman without fear.

But let's look deeper. Who would challenge danger like that unless fear were an issue in her life? People often chase the danger they're least afraid of to distract them from the part of life that scares them most.

Mary grew up in one of those high-power, high-pressure families. Her parents were incredibly judgmental about anything she did that didn't show excellence and ambition. They constantly dangled the carrot of their approval in front of her, but rarely let her have a nibble. She was starving for approval, and like all starving people she was terrified of not getting what she was hungry for. So Mary spent her life living up to what she imagined were other people's expectations.

That's why Mary became a lawyer. There had been prominent Boston lawyers in her family for generations. The family pressure had been relentless. If Mary didn't become a lawyer, worlds would crumble.

So the truth is that Mary's whole life had been governed by fear. Plunging into high-intensity activity that she didn't really find all that scary was the only way she could hide from the force that really scared her: people's disapproval. But when she almost died alone at sea, completely helpless, she realized, *So that's what a truly pitiless, overwhelming force is like. Any force less than that is nothing to be afraid of.*

Nearly dying at sea was a terrible ordeal. But the reason this happened was so that Mary could get a wonderful gift: the knowledge that she could live her life the way she wanted to, unafraid at last.

A Life Without Fear

When we discover the meaning of the events in our lives, it's always to complete our growth. Many of us need to grow in the direction of living without crippling fear. Isn't that the point of all education, not just Cosmic Kindergarten? You learn to read so you're not afraid to read anything that's presented to you, no matter how difficult. You learn to write so you're not afraid of any writing task that comes your way. And the more you learn, the more you learn *how* to learn so that when you're faced with having to master some new piece of knowledge, that, too, doesn't scare you.

Like Mary, many of us didn't get what we need so we can live without fear. And, by the way, when I talk about living without fear I'm not talking about the little phobias many of us have. You know—spiders, snakes, heights. These aren't usually such a big deal. We can work around them without distorting our lives. The fear I'm talking about that plagues so many of us is the kind that hijacks our life and carries it off into a direction we don't really want to go. I'm talking about fear of rejection, for example, so we live alone even though we hunger for contact. Or fear of failure, so we lead impoverished lives even though we hunger for accomplishment.

What does it take to produce people whose lives are governed by fear like this? Unfortunately, it's all too easy. You fill them with dread, while denying them the experiences necessary to make them feel that they can cope with what they're dreading.

Mary was constantly threatened with some terrible disapproval, but she never got a chance to learn to cope with that disapproval. Coping with that storm at sea put any amount of disapproval in perspective.

No matter what it is, if some event in your life leaves you desperately hungry to understand why it happened, the answer might be that it happened to help you let go of fear and find courage. If you want to know if this reason fits you, please answer the following diagnostic questions:

+ Is it hard for you to trust yourself to deal with new situations?

+ Think about a couple of the things you've done in your life that you regret. Was the main reason you did those things because you were acting out of fear?

- When you make a decision, is fear an important factor that you weigh in the balance?
- Would you say that your life is filled with things you're scared of?

If you answered *yes* to three or more of these questions, then the reason you went through what you did was to give you something that would make it possible to stop being afraid. Afraid of what? *Afraid of anything.*

Maybe what happened was that a cousin you were close to was killed in a senseless car crash. Or maybe your child was born very sick. Or maybe your spouse walked out on you. But everything happens for a reason.

The way to understand the gift the cosmos is offering you is by understanding just what gift you need to receive. If fear is a deep issue for you, then the meaning of what happened to you was to give you what you need to let go of fear.

Letting Go

Now you might be thinking, *Okay, I get it so far. But how did I get what I needed so I can let go of my fear?*

Realize that *the catastrophe has already happened.* Yet you survived. You're still intact. Although you may not have realized it at first, the experience of facing your catastrophe eventually forces you to see that your fear is irrelevant. You've been given a gift designed to help transport you outside the realm of fear.

It doesn't have to be complicated. Sometimes you just look and you can see it easily. Let me tell you what Jeff, a senior investigator for a major police force, told me.

"I had kind of a crummy childhood. My father left us. And my mother was this hippie nut. I mean, she couldn't cope, she couldn't earn money, she just dragged us around the country from place to place. I had to basically be the parent to my younger sister but there was no one to be my parent. I don't think I ever *had* a childhood, really. But it's funny. In a way I've always known why that happened. It all had to do with fear. My childhood was every scary thing a child can imagine, but I had to deal with it, and I did.

"For example, when I was fourteen I got home from school one day and I could immediately tell there was some kind of big trouble. My mother was drunk and scared. I just had the sense we had to get out of there fast. Stuff like this had happened before. I packed us up, I got my mother in the car, and I drove—remember I was fourteen—to my sister's school so we could pick her up. Then we got on the highway and headed out of state. I drove until my mother sobered up enough to drive. It turned out that she'd borrowed money from these real bad guys. For all I know they would've sold us all into prostitution to get back what they were owed.

"But I've always known that those years were a wonderful gift in some way. I saw over and over again that I never had to be afraid after that. Never, ever. I've been, well, pretty much fearless my whole life."

Now apply this to yourself. Here are some examples.

If your child was born sick, the catastrophe has already happened. Now you know what's really important in life. Now you know how strong you are. Now you've been given what you need to let go of needless fears.

If a cousin you were close to was killed in a senseless car crash, the catastrophe has already happened. You could spend the rest of your life afraid, but now that you know how precious life is you can see how important it is to live your life without fear. This perspective is what you needed to let go of your fear.

If your spouse walked out on you, the catastrophe has already happened. You know what it's like to live with a sword hanging over your head, and you know it's not worth living like that. Your new understanding allows you to stop being afraid.

Here's a story that illustrates in depth just how this happens.

Does Anyone Have Any Fortune Cookies?

Steve was thirty-seven, a handsome guy who looked forlorn, like a man who's lost his dog. After college, he'd gotten a grant that made it possible for him to travel around the world for a couple of years studying runaways, kids as young as seven who live on the streets of cities like São Paulo and Calcutta. Steve wanted to find out how these kids survived.

When he returned home he was seized with the idea of writing a novel based on what he'd seen, and he worked in a bookstore to support himself while he wrote. A decade later he'd written two long, searing novels filled with anger at a world that didn't want the worst parts of life shoved in its face. He couldn't get them published.

"I know I have to come to terms with the fact that I've wasted my youth," Steve said. "Just wasted it. That's my catastrophe. Now I have to move on. But I can't because it doesn't make any sense. It's too big a mistake to ignore. *It just has to make some sense.* There's got to be a reason in terms of something I've learned, maybe, or something I got that I wouldn't have gotten any other way. Because the only reason I have now is a bad one: that there's something wrong with me. And I can't live with that. I mean, it's like I can't go on thinking that I'm the kind of a guy who'd throw his whole youth away without building anything. So what does it mean? Do you have any fortune cookies?"

Steve answered the four diagnostic questions I just gave you. He came up with four strong *yes*es. I told him that the meaning of what happened to him was getting what he needed to let go of his fear.

Steve got lost in thought. Finally he said, "I don't know. There were so many parts of life I thought were stupid, and they made me very angry. I was going to stay above it all and write brilliant novels. That was ten years ago. That's when you're supposed to say, *Okay, this isn't working,* and you move on to something else. But I didn't move on. And after those first couple of years I think I knew that the reason I was continuing to waste my time was because I really was afraid of life. I was afraid I wasn't good enough. I was afraid I would just break apart in the face of the difficulties of life and show myself to be a very small, mediocre person. So you're right, Mira. I think I am afraid of everything. But how can overcoming my fears be the reason why I wasted so many years of my life?"

I asked Steve to tell me something specific he'd been afraid of.

"Well, I was afraid of going to work for some big corporation."

"Okay. What were you afraid would happen there?"

"I'd just, you know, not do well, not fit in, not be happy. It would be a disaster." There was a note of false bravado in his voice as he answered my questions, as if he were laughing off a catastrophe that really terrified him.

"And then what?"

"Eventually they'd fire me, I guess."

"And what would happen then?"

"Well, it would've all been such a waste and I'd feel terrible."

I paused. "Isn't that where you are now?" I said almost in a whisper.

Steve looked at me with incredible feeling in his eyes. "It's exactly where I am now," he said in a low husky voice, his bravado crumbling.

"That was the point," I said softly. "Everything you were afraid of has already happened. There's nothing more to be afraid of."

"So . . . so you're saying that the reason I wasted my life—so far anyway—was to see that I didn't have to be afraid of wasting my life?"

"Isn't that what makes us scared of anything?" I said. "You were scared; now it happened; now you see that you *can* cope. I mean, I see you standing here. You don't look like a basket case. And you're not alone in your situation. Lots of people can't move forward in life until the thing they're most afraid of happens to them and liberates them from their fear."

Steve got up from the chair he'd been sitting in. He started pacing around the room the way people sometimes do when they have something big to chew on. I could tell he was on the verge of saying something. Then he came over to his chair, put his hands on the back of it, and leaned forward.

"Let me tell you about my father. He was one of those Korean War guys. When he got out, he worked as a technician in the defense industry. Companies would keep losing a contract and my dad would keep getting laid off. As he got older and his skills got old, it was harder and harder for him to get a job. He worked incredibly hard, but instead of getting ahead he always kept falling behind. It broke his spirit. My father's life scared the crap out of me. You really can waste an entire life. And to do that working at a job you don't really care about . . . how could I not be scared?" Steve sighed. "You're right. My fear was controlling my life and I didn't even know it. I had to live my fear to loosen the grip it had on me."

Moving Forward with Courage

Steve had figured out how Cosmic Kindergarten works. We go through something tough and then we see what a gift it was because it made our fears irrelevant. But you can't stop there. The bigger the event, the bigger the gift. The bigger the gift, the more of a difference it has to make.

I know you still feel the same. But because of what happened to you, you have already conquered your fear in a way: You've been given exactly what you need to conquer your fear. You have to trust that.

Even though you may still feel the same old fears, you have to live as if those fears were now dead and gone. You've been given a gift that makes it possible to live without fear. Wow!

So what would you do if you really felt no fear? This question is the key to figuring out how to use what you've learned. There's some way fear kept you out of life. Seeing that you don't have to be afraid anymore gets you back into life. Whatever you do, it has to be something you couldn't allow yourself to do when you were afraid. Maybe you need to add something to your life. Or let something go from your life. Or do what you've been doing but in a different way.

When you make some change in your life because you believe you've been given the gift of letting go of fear, you'll really understand the meaning of what you went through.

And the Opposite of Fear Is . . .

Once you see that the reason something happened was so you could let go of fear, fear becomes different in your life. You realize it's more of a habit than a truth about the world. But it's a sticky habit. So how do you get out of the fear habit once you realize you no longer need it?

What you need is a better story about yourself. Your old story had to do with how afraid you were. *Your new story will have to do with how resilient you are.*

One woman I interviewed was caught in a college dorm fire in the middle of the night. It was terrifying. She managed to wake up her friends and get all of them out. However, she suffered serious smoke inhalation in the process.

Suppose this had happened to you. Looked at from the point of view of the old fear habit, this event shows how things can go wrong and you can get hurt. The light goes on when you see a completely different image of yourself in the same experience. Something bad happened and you survived. More—you came through like a champ, although it was very hard at the time. Now it's a story of your resilience. When people see that the meaning of what happened to them is that they no longer have to be afraid, they switch from seeing themselves as scaredy-cats to seeing themselves as resilient: less like victims, more like heroes.

Look back on some time in your life when you felt a lot of fear. Now tell yourself the story of what you went through, but this time make it a story about your resilience.

It's important to see that resilience doesn't stop with survival. It can take a person farther than he or she ever dreamed possible. At twenty-eight, Artie was diagnosed with multiple sclerosis. He came to me terrified of what the future held and hungry to know why this had happened to him. His answers to the diagnostic questions on pages 92–93 showed clearly that the reason this had happened was to help him let go of fear, which had been an issue in his life long before he got sick.

I asked him, "What would you do if you weren't afraid of the future?"

Actions speak louder than words. He'd never been particularly active before, but he started a program of running. At first this was primarily to maintain his muscle tone. But soon he decided that there was more here for him than this. He began running longer distances more often and faster. Eventually he started running in 10Ks and marathons. He took a survival reaction to a whole other level. He was inspired to add a new dimension to his life. His sense of himself as a physical being actually grew in spite of his disease. He no longer had to be afraid not only because he survived, but because he found a way to thrive more than he'd ever imagined.

Of course, we all die in the end. So are you going to wait until you're very old, and as you slip through the portals of death see that death itself is nothing to dread, *and then realize what a waste your lifetime of fear was?* You don't need to. For you, the catastrophe has already happened.

We all get to the point where we see that fear does nothing more than add an unnecessary element of pain to the process of living. We understand that terrorists win if we live with the fears they're trying to stir up. Well, we become terrorists to ourselves when we allow ourselves to be controlled by our own fears.

But Isn't Fear Your Friend?

Someone once asked me, "What's so terrible about fear? I mean, it's natural. Isn't fear a signal that you need to be careful? What's that thing they say about old, bold soldiers? There are old soldiers and there are bold soldiers, but there are no old, bold soldiers. Isn't that true?"

One of fear's oldest arguments is "I'll keep you safe." You've gotten a gift to help you let go of fear. You know that because of your answers to the diagnostic questions in this chapter. That gift was the meaning of what happened to you—something that's made it possible for you to find your courage. If you want to make use of this gift, you have to understand that "I'll keep you safe" is one of fear's greatest lies. Fear doesn't keep you safe. *Prudence* keeps you safe.

Former Israeli prime minister Ehud Barak faced this issue head-on. He had been the leader of an elite commando unit that faced the riskiest, most difficult assignments. He found that you cannot live a life like that with fear. The stress would kill you. Yet you'd think that without fear, your recklessness would kill you. So how do you survive?

Barak said, "The ability to survive [in a commando unit] is based on very careful planning and very careful behavior. When you're walking very close to the edge of a cliff, you have to behave in a very risk-averse way. I told my people, 'We are not adventurers! . . .' So you can walk very close to the edge of a cliff—if you make sure that every step is stable."

Before it was your panicky heart that kept you from danger. But it also gave you a limited life filled with pain. Now it's your cool head that will keep you from danger. Even without fear, you don't want to fall off the cliff. So think about what you're doing. Your mindfulness will keep you safe.

In any case, fear never really helps. Think about the fear we sometimes bring to relationships, how it makes us clutch, withdraw, and lash out. Then we always create the very thing we were afraid of. This happens everywhere fear operates.

What is it like to live without fear? Here's what two people said who've faced the worst kind of danger. Brad Wieners in "Gargoyles over Manhattan" said, "All experienced climbers know about this: the more you grip, the sooner you tire, and the more prone you are to falling." Peter Matthiessen put it more poetically in *The Snow Leopard*: "And of course it is this clinging, the tightness of panic, that gets people killed: 'to clutch,' in ancient Egyptian, 'to clutch the mountain,' in Assyrian, were euphemisms that signified 'to die.'"

Barak reminds us that it's all about being careful, not about being afraid. Wieners and Matthiessen remind us that being careful must go hand in hand with a certain relaxed attitude: careful but not clutching. That's what people who've faced the worst kind of danger can teach us about living without fear.

As you accept the gift of courage and think about what it means for you, remember that you can be careful without clutching and you'll be fine.

Death to a Bad Habit

Fear is a special issue. It's not only true that showing us a way to end fear is one of the ten reasons why things happen. But *all* ten of the reasons that things happen work in one way or another to end our fear: fear of not being loved, fear of not being strong, fear of not being happy, and so on. So it's important to make sure that we do everything possible to get what we need to end our fear.

At one point in our work together, one of my patients said something very smart. "It's been blowing my mind thinking that the reason I lived through what I did is so I could face my worst fear and give myself what I needed to move on. My question is this. Fear's been a habit for me. What do I do if fear creeps back in?"

Fear *is* a habit. What people don't realize is that it's one of the more curable habits. Think of it like this: When we get scared, we have thoughts that blow up a balloon of fear: *I'm going to die. Everything's ruined forever now. They will think I'm ridiculous now.* People who cope well with fear have counterthoughts that puncture holes in this balloon until all their fear leaks out. How do you do that? You use the patented Kirshenbaum Seven-Step Method for Overcoming Fear. All that's required is that you ask yourself seven questions.

1. *What am I really afraid of?* This is not a stupid question. Sometimes we know, but lots of times we don't. In your battle with fear you have to understand something: Fear tries to make itself as amorphous and vague as possible. That's how it gains power over you. Let's say you're starting a new relationship. Fear wants you to be "afraid it won't work out." Then your head is filled with nameless phantoms, and fear wins. *You* win when you get really specific. *Exactly* how and why wouldn't it work out? Because you're not right for each other? Okay, give your relationship enough time to see if you're right for each other. Then you win because the more specific a fear it is, the more easily it can be conquered because it's *smaller.*

2. *What's the worst that can happen?* Many times we're afraid because we've panicked ourselves unnecessarily. There's simply no point in being afraid if, once you've looked into it, the worst that can happen isn't really something so terrible. Lots of people are terrified of speaking in public, for example. Well, suppose you have to speak at the next meeting of your school's PTA. What's the worst that can happen? You won't make such

a great speech. You'll hesitate, lose your place, have to be asked to speak more loudly . . . and so what? The worst thing that happened was that as an amateur speaker you came across like an amateur. So what? You don't speak in public for a living. You're just a parent.

3. *How likely is it?* Many of us when we fly are afraid of the plane crashing, for example. But how likely is it? It turns out that it's very unlikely. *There are five thousand flights a day in the United States alone.* Many of the things we're afraid of lose their power to scare us when we realize how unlikely they are to happen. People who are good at dealing with fear have the habit of asking the question "How likely is it to happen?" and then coming up with a realistic answer (usually, "Pretty darned unlikely") and then getting comfort from that answer.

4. *Can I prevent this?* It turns out that if we spend a little less time sucking the thumb of fear and a little more time thinking about what we can do to take care of ourselves, the need for fear shrinks enormously. This is what we mean by prudence. This is why we say a stitch in time saves nine or an ounce of prevention is worth a pound of cure.

Admittedly there's nothing you can do to prevent a giant asteroid from crashing into the earth. But most of the things we're afraid of are much more preventable than this. Most people are scared of cancer, for example. And while it's true that everyone is going to die of something, cancer is actually one of the more preventable diseases, particularly when you factor in the way early detection prevents cancer from being fatal.

5. *Can I insure myself against this?* I'm not talking about the kind of insurance you buy. Insurance just means you do something so that if the thing you're afraid of happens, you'll still be okay. Take someone in a relationship who's afraid of being dumped. Sometimes a person blows off her friends when she's in a relationship. Well, then, who's going to be there for her if she does get dumped? Maintaining a strong bond with your friends is a way to give yourself insurance in case your relationship doesn't work out. And there are always things we can do to give ourselves some insurance no matter what we're afraid of.

6. *Could I cope with it if the thing I'm afraid of came to pass?* We get so panicky we fail to realize that if the thing we're afraid of happened, we'd actually be able to cope rather well.

   Suppose you get laid off. We say things like "This would be devastating. I don't know what I'd do." Notice how we use words that create their own panic. But come on. You'll look for another job, won't you? And with time and some help you'll find one, won't you? The point is, assume the best about your ability to cope, not the worst, because most people can actually cope much better than they think they can.

7. *Who can I talk to about this?* One of the worst parts of fear comes when you try to keep it to yourself. Don't. Share it with someone you trust. You can even share it with strangers. If you're making a speech and you're scared to death, for example, tell the audience you're nervous. They'll be much more accepting, and you'll be amazed at how much your being open calms your own fear.

Each one of these fear-killing questions is a dart that has the power to puncture your balloon of fear. Taken all together, these questions are a complete kit of darts that should enable you to puncture any balloon of fear. Ask the questions. Really think about your answers. And then watch the balloon of fear shrink to nothing.

Tying Balloons to a Stone

———◆◆◆———

Forgiveness, schmorgiveness, right? So you don't forgive the people in your life who've hurt you. So what? Who cares? Why should this be a big deal?

Well, let me tell you about a couple I'm working with right now. They've been married for fourteen years. One night in their first year of marriage they made love in a way that was very unsatisfying to the woman. It was late, they were both tired, she admittedly was in a bad mood, and the previous time they'd made love it hadn't been so great for her either. So that night she said something to her husband about his being a lousy lover with a small penis: "You don't have much to work with, and you can't do much with it"—words to that effect. She didn't really mean it, but she said it.

Naturally he was very hurt. He was particularly hurt

because there was some truth to what his wife had said, and he knew that she'd intended to hurt him. He could never forgive her. His old spontaneous desire to make love to her evaporated. They almost never had sex unless she initiated it, so she stopped feeling that he desired her. And he really did stop desiring her, the way you stop wanting to put your hand on a hot stove. Unforgiveness ate away at their love like termites on a house of twigs.

Let me get right to the diagnostic questions:

+ Do you think a lot about some of the ways you've been hurt or about disappointments you've suffered in the past?
+ Do you get angry a lot or have you been holding onto your anger for a long time?
+ Is feeling guilty very much an issue for you?
+ Do you spend time having "if only" fantasies where you think about how your life would be different now if you or someone else had done things differently in the past?
+ Do you often feel envious?
+ In some important way, do you not feel safe or secure in your life?

If you answered *yes* to three or more of these questions, then the reason you went through what you did was for you to get what you needed to forgive yourself or someone else; really forgive, not just say the words. The forgiveness that has eluded you is now possible.

If this applies to you, you've been given a real gift. You see, not being able to forgive wouldn't be such a big deal if it were like an old debt. You know, someone from a million years ago

MIRA KIRSHENBAUM

borrowed a hundred bucks from you, and you lost track of that person and, yeah, you remember the debt and you'd like your money back but it doesn't cost you anything to carry that memory around with you in the back of your mind. There's no *feeling* attached to it.

But the inability to forgive is not like that. It's a poison. After all, what was done to you was a big deal on some level if it's so hard for you to forgive. Maybe you were humiliated. But as you live not forgiving the other person, you keep rehearsing that humiliation over and over in your mind, and just when its embers are about to die out you fan the flame and feel your humiliation yet again. You're drinking the poison of humiliation. Maybe the other person did something that betrayed a trust. Now, like someone terrified of being hurt, you search for ways you're vulnerable and add up your fears like a miser counting his coins. All this does is force you to think about how insecure you are, and so you poison yourself with fear.

It poisons you just as much if most of the time it simmers outside of your awareness. You know that because of the heat it brings every time it resurfaces.

No one intends to be unforgiving. In our society it's more something we feel we "can't help" than something we're proud of. But that's the point. It really does seem like something we can't help. We're just stuck with it, like someone with an abscessed tooth and no dentist to provide relief. But don't imagine only how painful that would be. Imagine how you wouldn't be able to live a normal life with such a toothache. That's what happens when we're stuck unable to forgive someone else or when we can't forgive ourselves.

We see this every time we open the newspapers these days. Almost every troubled part of the world is a place where violence feeds on unforgiveness. The cycle of violence is utterly dependent on the inability to forgive. Our world is deformed by unforgiveness.

The End of Blame

Part of what can make it so hard for us to forgive is the automatic way we orient ourselves in life through blame. If anything goes wrong anywhere, the first thing anyone thinks about is who to blame. It's like when you smell a fart in an elevator— the first thing you want to know is *Who did it?* Blame is a very deep instinct because it makes us feel safe. If the mortality rate in a hospital goes up, you figure out who or what to blame and the rate goes down again. If there's a terrorist attack but you can figure out who to blame, then you can start feeling safe from terrorists. That series of links—disaster, blame, safety— is hardwired into us.

Blame is the match that ignites unforgiveness. And why can't we forgive? After all, a lot of the time we do. When someone accidentally steps on your toe while you're waiting in line at the bank, he or she turns around and profusely apologizes. And what do you say? "Oh, it was nothing." But when we can't forgive it's because we can't bring ourselves to say, "It was nothing," about this particular thing that was done to us. It was too big, too hurtful. To say that it was nothing would be like saying that *we're* nothing, and we can't do that. We can't forgive when it feels like forgiveness involves the annihilation of the

111

self. So it seems like we're doomed to carry around the poison of unforgiveness. We're trapped in it.

No wonder we sometimes need a huge event to shake us loose from the inability to forgive. This may, in fact, be the meaning of some event in your life. Maybe something happened to you a long time ago and its meaning has been a mystery, like finding a key in a drawer in a dead relative's house and wondering what special lock this key is meant to open since the key seemed so carefully put away. Yet that event has been the key you've needed to set yourself free from your inability to forgive.

If forgiveness is in store for you, and I hope it is, it might help to know what it feels like. After all, some of us wouldn't recognize forgiveness if it bit us in the ankle.

The Gift of Forgiveness

What does forgiveness actually feel like? I'll tell you this much: It feels very different for people who actually can forgive than it does for people who haven't yet been able to forgive. When you can't forgive, you focus on being able to say, "I forgive you." This either seems like nothing, mere words, or else it seems like this impossible act of magic that goes far beyond anything you think is real—as if forgiveness could happen simply because you say it's happening. Maybe a priest can do that, but not civilians.

Now here's how it works when people really do forgive. Let's say someone hurt you. Your sister took your boyfriend away from you. Your coworker stole an idea of yours and got the credit for it. Ouch! Now imagine that the unforgiveness you feel has been a heavy stone that lies right on your chest. When you actually forgive, it will be as if there's a cluster of helium balloons that lifts that stone away. There are different balloons because forgiveness achieves liftoff as a result of different ingredients—different thoughts, reasons, and feelings. You tie one balloon to the stone and maybe nothing happens. You tie another to it. Still nothing. But then maybe you tie a third helium balloon to the stone and up it rises. Houston, we have liftoff. Forgiveness has happened. Your *reasons* to forgive have finally picked up your unforgiveness and floated it away.

What are these helium balloons that create forgiveness?

- Sometimes anger just runs its course and dies, and we need to be made aware of that fact.
- Sometimes we actually forget what happened.
- Sometimes we come to have a better understanding of why people acted the way they did.
- Sometimes we grow to care a lot less about what happened.
- Sometimes we're made aware of how our lack of forgiveness is hurting us.
- Sometimes enough good things have happened so that trust is rebuilt with the person who hurt us.

When some event in your life shakes you up to the point where you can find forgiveness, it does so by giving you just enough of the right helium balloons to lift that stone off your chest.

Let me tell you about Doug, who had a big problem with forgiveness. His story will show you how to use what happened to you to get to the point where you can forgive.

The Lost Boy

Doug, forty-six, was a handsome Steve Martin look-alike who ran an ad agency. His words came out like a dam burst. I see this a lot with people who are good talkers but who have some huge, heavy problem they've kept secret from everyone.

"It's quite a story," Doug said. "I have an eighteen-year-old son, Dougie. Four years ago he started getting involved with some really bad kids and drugs. He was such a great little guy and then in like two weeks he was suddenly this total druggie. We did everything you can imagine: hospitals, rehab. And then he got arrested for dealing and we had to cope with that. Thank God he was a juvenile. He never wanted help.

"That nightmare went on and on for years. Then six months ago he disappeared. We've hired detectives. The police have done whatever the hell they do. I think he's just gotten lost in some crack house in New York or L.A. or God knows where. I just hope he's not dead.

"But sometimes I think it would almost be better if he were. Then at least I'd know what was what. What I hate about this whole thing is the uncertainty. All I know is that Dougie's probably out there and if he is he needs my help. But I can't do anything. I never could do anything to help him since he started getting in trouble with drugs. That's why I've got to find some meaning in this. It can't all be for nothing—that I raised this beautiful child and he becomes nothing but a misery to himself and a burden to everyone else.

"I'll tell you one thing: I can't work. People aren't going to be able to cover for me at the agency for much longer. I need some positive meaning for this that makes sense so I can move on. I realize all too well these stories don't always have happy endings. Then what?"

I asked Doug the diagnostic questions I asked you earlier in this chapter.

"Wow," he said, "those questions really hit me. I had a big *yes* for almost every single one. I guess this applies to me big time. And that's odd because I haven't seen forgiveness as something I need to work on. I think, yeah, I need to forgive myself for what's happened to my son, but . . . well, it just can't be that the reason that my son got into trouble was so I could forgive myself for the role I played in his getting into trouble. That would just be weird."

"Yes," I said, "you're absolutely right. The reason someone fell off a ladder and broke a leg can't be so he could forgive himself for falling off the ladder. If getting to forgiveness was the reason the guy fell off the ladder and broke his leg, it was forgiveness for something that happened much earlier and perhaps was a lot bigger, like maybe the way his older brother had been so busy when he was growing up and had treated him like a pest. Then the guy falls off the ladder and realizes, *Hey, people get busy, they get distracted, and there's no way they can avoid making mistakes. So maybe I can finally forgive my brother.*

"So I'm sure," I went on, "your need for forgiveness started well before all this happened with your son. Who were you blaming before all this happened? Follow the blame and you'll find the person you need to forgive."

"The first thing that comes to mind is my father," Doug said. "He was a mean bastard, cold and judgmental. Nothing I did was ever good enough. Like the time in the tenth grade when I finally got a report card with all As and Bs, no Cs. I brought it home and all my father said was 'Okay, now next time you can get all As.'" Doug's voice was getting husky. This was very emotional for him.

"And you've never forgiven him," I said.

"You're right. I've never forgiven him. I call him on the phone every week. When we talk sometimes I act like I don't care about him, more to punish him than to liberate myself, like *Ha! See, I don't care about you.* But of course I've never forgiven him."

"So how's that working out for you?"

"I don't know. It hasn't killed me. Look . . . what would I even say? *I forgive you?* It would just be words."

We were silent for a moment. Then I said, "You think it keeps you strong, not being able to forgive your father, like it protects you from his mojo. But I think it's hurting you a lot. The anger and the memory of the pain you carry around are an unhealed wound."

"So what does it really mean to forgive someone?" Doug asked.

The Face of Forgiveness

What *does* it mean to forgive someone? Good question. "If you have someone visiting your house and he or she breaks a vase you really like, at some point you get some perspective on the whole thing, and you say, *What the hell, people knock things over, it's just a vase, this person is a friend.* It's not that you're minimizing the loss. But no vase is worth a friendship, and nothing we could possibly lose is bigger than life itself. You're not doing justice to yourself unless you see that forgiveness restores your life to you. When you forgive, you're saying to the cosmos and, most of all, to yourself, that you're okay now. When you can't forgive it's like you're proclaiming that you're not okay, and *saying* you're not okay somehow undermines you and *makes* you not okay."

"So you're saying I need to get perspective so I can find forgiveness?" Doug asked.

"Sure. Look at your answers to the questions. People who answer these questions the way you did eventually said that the reason they went through what they did was to get the perspective that would enable them to find forgiveness. And where does that perspective come from? *From the event itself.*"

If you can figure out how to forgive yourself or the person responsible for the bad thing that happened to you, then that will be the very same reason why you need to forgive the person from your past.

This is an amazing thing to say, but it's true.

"Remember the guy who fell off the ladder? What was the meaning of that fall for him? So he could forgive his brother. How? Well, how did he forgive himself for falling? He said, *You get busy, you get distracted, you make mistakes.* Well, that's the very same reason he has to forgive his brother.

"It's almost as if the events in our lives can be a very specific lesson in forgiveness. There's meaning in what happened with your son, and the meaning is that you've been given a way to forgive your father. How? *If you see how to forgive yourself for what happened to your son, you'll see how to forgive your father.*"

"I guess I'd probably say that I did my best and it wasn't my responsibility that Dougie was the way he was."

"I'll bet that's exactly what you'll say. And that's the gift in this experience for you. This is just what you need to say about your father to be able to forgive him."

"You're telling me I'm going to have to say he did his best and ultimately he doesn't deserve praise or blame for how I turned out?!?!"

"That's it. Exactly. Things happen to us to teach us a very specific lesson in forgiveness. I'll tell you this. Until you find the forgiveness that's now possible for you, your life is going to stink."

"My life already stinks," Doug blurted out.

"*The reason this thing happened with your son is to help you find a way to make your life not stink,*" I said as emphatically as I could. "It's to wake you up to the possibility that there's something else besides blame. If you're more accepting now of yourself, of other people, and of the things that happen in life, you can have a good life. And that will take you to a happy future. And *that* will heal your disappointed past. When was the last time you looked forward to the future? I'm talking about before all this stuff happened with your son."

Doug looked stunned. "I've never looked forward to the future. I've *worried* about the future. That's how I've felt safe. You sort of worry your way toward a good future." There was a pause. "That's what my father did. What I saw from the outside must have felt very different to him from the inside. Maybe he didn't feel he was being a mean bastard. Maybe he just felt he was worrying me toward what he felt would be a good future for me."

"Maybe the best gift you can give your son is to let go of all the blame so he can come back to a blame-free atmosphere. That's what forgiveness is anyway—a blame-free environment."

"What do I say, my dad was just a guy like every other guy going back to Adam? It feels so . . . nothing."

"But you have to do it. And here's why."

Paper, Stone, and Scissors

"Look, Doug," I continued, "I'm sure you've let go of things in your life. Okay, now quick, give me the first answer that comes into your head: If all this time and energy you've spent with blame were freed up, why would that be a gift? What would it be good for?"

Just as I asked him to, Doug didn't hesitate. "I need to find love. I got divorced about six years ago. My wife said I was a mean bastard. I've gone out with a lot of women since then and it's never worked. I think it's never worked because I'm very critical and they don't like me because they think I don't like them."

"Blame kills love," I said. "It's like when you play paper, stone, and scissors. Paper beats stone. Some people don't get that, because a stone is tougher than paper. But the paper can wrap itself around the stone and make it disappear. That's what blame does to love, and it happens in your heart."

"So I should stop blaming my father."

"He *was* just a father like a million other fathers, based on what you've told me. But maybe there was something about having a father who was a tough guy that gave you a certain

119

toughness you need for running an ad agency, which must be a complete zoo."

"It's a total zoo. But I love it."

"It's the only place in your life where there's no blame."

"Wow. That's right. Maybe that's why I love it so much. So I have to forgive."

"Exactly," I said. "So, when you find a way to forgive yourself, it will show you a way to forgive your father. Can you do that, Doug?"

"I don't know. I'm just so tired of all this blame and carrying grudges and everything. But how do I forgive myself?"

"You get tired of not forgiving. You realize what a burden it's been. And you just put it down, like letting yourself go to sleep. There's nothing to go out and *do*. It just happens because there are so many good reasons for it to happen, the way you let yourself fall asleep when there are so many good reasons for you to fall asleep. It can feel impossible, and then suddenly it just happens."

For Doug it was an event in his present (his son's problems) whose meaning enabled him to find forgiveness for something that happened in his past (the way his father had treated him). Now let's meet Ellen. For her it was the opposite. It was an event from her past whose meaning enabled her to find forgiveness for things that were happening in her present.

A Hank of Hair and a Bag of Bones

Ellen, thirty-seven, came to me because her problems with forgiveness were interfering with her work. Ellen was a psychiatric nurse. Too many of the people who came into her hospital reminded her painfully of her own problems, and she responded with impatience instead of understanding. Here's what she told me.

"Back in my teens and twenties I had this monster case of anorexia. I made Karen Carpenter look like Dom DeLuise. For years I looked like a hank of hair and a bag of bones. I went into cardiac arrest a couple of times. The whole thing practically killed my parents. It was really bad. And I don't really know how I came out of it. I didn't suddenly 'realize' something I'd never realized before. It was more like one day they said you've got to eat your potatoes like they'd done a million times and that day I just ate the damned potatoes. And I never looked back. To me that's creepy because . . . am I cured, or what happened?

"On some level I've moved on. I've been healthy for ten years and most of the time I never think about who that crazy girl was back then who worked so hard to destroy herself. But on another level that part of me is always there. You go forward and you're not thinking about it and when you least expect it something happens and *boom!* the whole thing is there like it was just yesterday."

"Can you give me an example?" I asked.

"Yeah, it sort of happens all the time. Patients keep coming in and most of the time I think I'm really good with them. But then we had, like, this young man—he was in medical school, things started getting overwhelming, and he tried to kill himself. And I felt so hostile toward him. When I asked him questions it would be like I was grilling him. It's always the self-destructive note in people that makes me so furious with them. I'm so hard on people then; merciless, really. I can't forgive people for their flaws. And this whole thing keeps ruining my life. I lived with this guy, Charlie, for about a year and a half. I really loved him and we were going to get married, but whenever he crossed some line I was so incredibly hard on him. He just couldn't take it. And I don't blame him."

"If you don't forgive yourself, you're going to be hard on everyone you care about and you're going to keep losing them. Why would anyone ever feel safe with you unless he felt there was forgiveness at your very core? The only guys who will stand for it are the ones who are so cold inside that they don't notice that your heart is filled with blame." Then I asked Ellen to answer the diagnostic questions in this chapter. She said *yes* to almost all of them.

"Your answers to the diagnostic questions show that there's meaning in what you went through," I said, "and the meaning lies in your being given the possibility of forgiveness. You needed to be given that possibility, and you were. At some point down the road you're going to be saying, 'The reason I went through such hell with my eating disorder was to really show me how important it is to be a forgiving person.' Because here's the thing: I don't think what happened to you made you such a hard-ass. I think you were born with that hard part of you fully developed. Do you think you could've starved yourself the way you did unless you had a tough component to your personality? I don't think so. What happened to you was your chance to learn to be more forgiving."

After a moment Ellen said, "Who or what do I really need to forgive?"

"If you see who you're blaming, you'll see who you need to forgive."

"I'm blaming myself."

"But which part of yourself?"

Another pause. "The sick part of myself."

"You were starving yourself partly because you couldn't stand your imperfections. Now you can't stand the imperfection that led you to anorexia. When you know what to blame, you know what to forgive. Imagine the unimaginable: you forgiving your imperfections. You know what?" I said, taking a risk. "I bet somewhere along the line you ran into someone who was a model for how you can forgive your imperfections."

Ellen got the idea immediately. "In one of the hospitals I was in there was this nurse who, I don't know, her approval of me didn't go up and down according to how much I ate that day. She was always kind to me. She saw a person inside of me beyond my disease. It was almost like she didn't care about my disease, just about the person I was. And in her eyes that person had nothing to do with my disease. I just loved her for that."

"It's almost like you got sick," I said, "so you could find this person who could teach you this lesson about self-forgiveness. After all, if you were so sick, you could only get that way if you were completely unforgiving of the slightest deviation from your plan because you weren't living up to some ideal. And then this woman showed you that you can forgive someone who isn't perfect, even if that person is yourself."

"I know what that woman did. I just don't know how to do that for myself." And she cried.

Paths to Forgiveness

Forgiveness is hard. But I'll tell you what I told Ellen: "I think forgiveness would be a lot easier except for the ways that the past keeps living in the present. It's fear that's preventing you from forgiving yourself, which is the way it is for most people. I think you still feel that that woman who tried to starve herself to death and came so close to succeeding is alive and well inside you. You don't know how to feel safe from that woman inside you.

"You're letting that woman you were define who you are now. But maybe there's a way to acknowledge what happened to you without letting it define you so much. You know, that *is* going to happen, anyway. You're still young. Ten, twenty years from now you're going to look at the life you've built and you're going to see how much your life comes from *you*, not the sick you, but the *you* you. That's what's going to define who you are. So why not do it sooner rather than later? And then when your old self isn't such a big deal in the story of your life, believe me, forgiveness is going to be a lot easier.

"There are many paths you can follow to forgiveness. That was one: *Understand that your present is different from your past.* Here's another: *Focus on how it's hurt you not to forgive yourself and on what you need to be safe.* It's hurt you, Ellen, because it's made you hard on everyone you should be caring about and that just drives them away. What you need to be safe is to see that you're not saved from anorexia because you're such a hard-ass. Being such a hard-ass was part of your anorexia. You're saved from anorexia because you're you, the you you've been these past ten years. Do you think your old self would ever have come to see me and try to come to terms with your need to forgive yourself?"

"So I'm here and that means I'm not like I was?"

"Just look at yourself. There are a thousand reasons why you're not like that sick skinny girl. What can I tell you? Let's keep looking for more reasons to forgive yourself."

"I've got one," Ellen said. "*Because I've suffered enough.* I was my own punishment. I just have to meditate on that and I think I should definitely be able to forgive myself."

"Yeah! I think if we realize how much the people we blame have suffered themselves, forgiveness would sweep the world. The thing is that you have to be forgiving of yourself as you go through the process of trying to find forgiveness. It's not like suddenly seeing the light. It's like, you tune in to that signal where you really do feel you can forgive yourself or another person. Then you lose it. You get the signal back again, and then you lose it, and then you get it back again. The signal keeps coming back stronger each time, and you get better at tuning in to it. It takes a while, but gradually your forgiveness takes over. Just be patient with yourself as you go through this zigzag process."

. . . and Watch It Float Away

Suppose your answers to the diagnostic questions show that the reason you went through some event in your life was to find forgiveness for something or someone. This means that being a forgiving person is an incomplete part of your development and that Cosmic Kindergarten has arranged for you to complete your lesson. Forgiveness is now a possibility for you. Here's how to achieve it.

First, look at the event itself, even if it seems to have absolutely nothing to do with forgiveness. Maybe you just fell off your bicycle. But look at that event carefully to see how forgiveness was possible there. The event Doug was trying to find meaning for was his son's addiction and disappearance. The forgiveness that was possible there was his seeing that he'd done his best as a father and that sometimes no matter what you do as a parent things turn out the way they turn out, for good or for bad.

Then apply this understanding to the event in your life for which you've not been able to find forgiveness. For Doug, it was not being able to forgive his father. But now he could see that his father, too, had done his best and that Doug had turned out the way he had pretty much regardless of what his father had done.

This understanding you've gained is nothing more than a reason to forgive. That's what your life has given you. Maybe that reason is enough. Imagine that the reason to forgive is a helium-filled balloon. Imagine tying that balloon to the stone of your unforgiveness. Maybe that reason is enough to lift the stone and float it away.

But maybe you need more reasons. Maybe one is not enough in itself, but together they're enough for liftoff. Here are some of the most powerful reasons people have found for forgiveness. Think about which ones make sense to you. Imagine tying all the ones that make sense to you to the stone of your unforgiveness.

Some people are able to forgive when they realize that the other person just couldn't help it, because he or she was sick, damaged, or limited somehow.

Some people find forgiveness when they realize the other person has suffered more than they have.

We also forgive when we realize the other person has suffered enough, even if he or she hasn't suffered more than we have.

We forgive when we realize we're safe now.

We forgive when we realize that we don't want to be the kind of person who doesn't forgive.

We forgive when the other person makes up for what he or she has done.

But perhaps the most important reason is that when we don't forgive, we're the ones who are hurt the most.

Buried Treasure

———◆◦◆◦———

We are often unaware of what's best in us—amazing talents we've never known we had. How did we miss them? Lots of things blind us to the treasure inside us: the demands of earning a living, limited opportunities when we're growing up. But while we don't know what treasures we have, we know that some piece of them is missing in our everyday lives. We know that we feel incomplete, unfulfilled.

This is how Monica felt when her world collapsed. She'd been a happily married stay-at-home mom with two kids in elementary school. She often volunteered at the school and sometimes helped out with paperwork at her husband's large auto-body-repair shop. She assumed her life was perfect. So she couldn't understand why she sometimes felt so restless and unhappy.

Then one day when she was out running errands she turned a corner and literally bumped into her old boyfriend from high school: the one who'd taken her to the senior prom; the one to whom she'd given her virginity. He was recently divorced, looking great, and happy to see her. They went out for a drink and said good-bye, but a few days later he called her up and they got together again. For some reason she found herself carefully avoiding telling her husband anything about this. She knew she was being drawn into something, and part of her wanted to be drawn into it.

Monica got together with her old boyfriend five times before her world blew up. All they'd done was talk and kiss good-bye. Monica didn't tell her husband about it because she knew how jealous he could be. That was her mistake: Given his jealousy, she should've told her husband something about what she was doing, since it was basically innocent, or just not done it. When he found out about it he refused to believe the truth, that nothing really had gone on between them. He kicked her out and divorced her.

To have her life destroyed for a small mistake felt so unfair to her.

That's how it feels when something bad happens to us. Out of all the people we know, we're the one who slipped on a banana peel, and now we're sitting there flat on our ass with nothing but pain to show for our adventure, and everyone's looking down at us, laughing. And how much worse it is when, like for Monica and for so many of us, the bad thing that's happened is the result of our own mistakes.

Still, in every fall like this there's a gift or opportunity. And it's just the one we were needing most in our lives. That gift or opportunity was the reason we fell.

Nothing shows this more clearly than when you go through tough times and it turns out they had meaning because you discovered buried treasure within yourself, some talent you never knew you had. It's like slipping on a banana peel, falling down, feeling some hard little thing poking into your ass, and discovering you've landed on a diamond. Now who's the loser? You're a winner. You went through something tough but you came away with something valuable.

What talent could this possibly be? It could be something as simple as finding out you're good at handling money. It could be that you're good at organizing things. It could be that you have more compassion than you ever imagined. It could be that you're great at creating and maintaining friendships. It could be that you have real artistic talent. It could be any talent at all.

That's what happened with Monica. She retained custody of her children, but even with the child support that her husband religiously paid, she had to earn a living. Like millions of other displaced homemakers, she hadn't worked in a long time and had few marketable skills. But from helping her husband she knew the business end of running an auto-body-repair shop. So Monica called around to every auto-body-repair shop in the city, offering to come in, sort out the paperwork, help with billing insurance companies, work at collecting monies owed. Many of these were small shops that had been struggling along by the seat of their pants. Some were willing to give Monica a try.

Over the next few years Monica built a tiny company that offered business services to very small outfits that could barely afford to outsource anything, but Monica's ace in the hole was that she focused on businesses that she figured had lots of accounts receivable. She essentially paid herself, and soon her part-time employees, from the monies she brought in. It was almost as if she were cost free from the businesses' point of view. It was a total win-win.

Now here's the good part. It was the part that Monica told me was the reason her life had seemed to collapse. It was to give her what she needed so she'd didn't feel incomplete and unfulfilled anymore. She had a talent for business. Solving problems, winning clients—all this made her feel she was coming into her own.

Although the stories may be very different, based on my research, helping us discover buried treasure within ourselves is one of the most common reasons that things happen to us. The world is filled with flesh-and-blood men and women who've gone through difficulties like ours, and with time and patience they've come to see that they really did land on a diamond when they fell on their ass.

Are you one of these people?

Please answer the following diagnostic questions:

- Have you felt for a long time that you're bigger than your life or better than the circumstances you find yourself in?

- Have you always suspected or wished you were special?

- When you were growing up, did you often feel disparaged for your intelligence or abilities?

- Have you found yourself saying *no* to opportunities because you're afraid you don't have what it takes to handle them?
- Do you feel that when you were younger you had talents or abilities that you're not in touch with now?

If you answer *yes* to three or more of these questions, the meaning of what happened to you was to help you uncover a hidden talent.

A Footprint in the Sand

Some of the most compelling stories that have held our attention for the longest throughout history have been stories of people discovering untapped talents within themselves as a result of loss and ordeal.

Take Robinson Crusoe. Talk about losing something. Robinson Crusoe lost everything, plus he was thrown onto an island with seemingly nothing on it.

Every version of this story has the same arc. First there's shock, helplessness, frustration, despair. But then there's a slow-to-dawn sense that you're not helpless, that you have much more to work with than you thought, that you can create a much nicer world for yourself than you ever imagined. You lost everything and found that *you* were so much more than you ever imagined. Talk about falling on your ass and landing on a diamond! Robinson Crusoe didn't find gold on his island, but he did find gold within himself, a whole new sense of what he was capable of.

Every story, real or made up, about someone going through

an ordeal has this element of discovering treasure within your-self beyond what you ever imagined.

One of the most inspiring stories like this is Helen Keller's. She was both deaf and blind in an age when there wasn't much understanding of either of these conditions. Yes, she too was in a sense a castaway, living on an island of darkness and silence. But having to deal with it—and she did have excellent help, the way Crusoe had Friday—revealed talents that might never have come to light if she hadn't had to struggle.

It's interesting how hungry we are for stories like this. Our hunger comes from the fact that we don't want to feel like los-ers. It's sad: When people search for a reason why something bad happened to them, some conclude that it's because they're a loser. People who get seriously ill, people who lose a loved one in an accident, anyone dogged by misfortune is susceptible to thinking about himself as a loser. I've heard people say, "It's like God put this invisible target on my back for the fates to take potshots at."

Using this label *loser* makes a certain psychological sense. When we see something bad happening to someone, it's very hard to think that we live in a universe where bad things like that happen for no reason whatsoever. That's an unbearable thought. So we blame the victim, and if we're the victim, we blame ourselves. Cancer? "I wasn't living right." Can't find a mate? "I must be doing something to deserve this loneliness." Job loss? "I'm lazy and stupid."

And why search for a specific reason when you can just say *loser?*

Well, I've got to tell you—when I say everything happens

for a reason, *loser* is not what I have in mind. It doesn't bring closure, hope, peace of mind, or the ability to move forward to think that you deserve your fate. The problem is that once that word *loser* gets in a person's head, he or she can't shake it by merely telling it to go away. Let's be honest. Life isn't fair. Some people lead charmed lives. Others seem to have more than their share of misfortune. If you can't blame someone else, it's hard not to fall back on blaming yourself and calling yourself a loser. But it's still vicious and *false*. And we all know it.

The loser label is deeply destructive. It causes people to stop trying and allow their world to shrink. This is the exact opposite of the direction in which we're supposed to move.

A person can reverse the shrinkage by seeing that every loss can also be an opportunity. This is a fact. And that opportunity very often lies in discovering a hidden talent.

Welcome to Josie's Place

How do you discern the talent that Cosmic Kindergarten arranged to be uncovered? I'll give you a hint: *It's what you do when you're shipwrecked on your desert island that reveals your talent*, just the way it was for Monica.

Difficulties always bring us to a new place in our lives. In the old place the talents we used were all too familiar, but they hogged the spotlight. The new place we're in always seems to require new talents, which is why it usually feels uncomfortable at first. You just need to trust that if you're active instead of passive in this new place, hopeful instead of despairing, your talent will come to light. But now you can have this trust, because you know how Cosmic Kindergarten works.

The following story will make this clear. Josie, forty-two, had owned a successful Italian restaurant. It was called, not surprisingly, Josie's Place. In her small suburban community miles outside of Boston, Josie's, the only Italian restaurant in the area, had been the place to go. Josie's was so successful that she got a bank loan, leased a storefront, and prepared to open a Josie's II in a nearby town. Unfortunately, all this happened before she knew that some chains were going to open in the area—an Olive Garden and a Bertucci's.

Just when Josie was facing a cash crunch, this competition knocked her out of the box. She went out of business and lost most of the money she'd invested.

Josie was one of the people who'd been pointed out to me as someone who'd been successful at discovering a positive meaning from a negative event. Here's what she said to me: "You know, when you drive around town you sometimes notice that someone's gone out of business—a gift shop, an ice cream parlor, or something. And you probably think—I know I do— *Gee, that's too bad.* But I don't think you fully appreciate what's really going on in a lot of these cases. An earthquake happened. Someone's whole world was shaken up. A home was destroyed. Those people's very future quivers on a fault. I know that's what it was like for me, losing my restaurants.

"Then there's that huge gap between where you were, puffed up with your hopes, and the ashes you're holding when it's all over. Compared to what you had, you feel like you have nothing, and you feel *like* a nothing. Sometimes I thought, *No, wait a minute, I really was a good businesswoman and I just fell victim to a huge piece of bad luck.* But that's not reassuring at all, because now you're thinking you're this person who walks around under a cloud with a target painted on her back.

"But that whole time I had a sense that there was a reason that my life had gone up in smoke the way it had; a damned good reason, too. You have these hints, little whisperings, just outside your consciousness. But you know they're there and you can follow them.

"For me these hints of what it meant that I went through what I did somehow had to do with my going to church. I was so lost in my life and I felt somehow I would find the answer in church. I always feel good in church anyway. I always feel good praying. But I'd always thought religion was mostly a gift for me. I never thought that I had a gift for religion."

This proved to be a turning point in Josie's life. Like so many talented people she'd always devalued her talents, like someone who doesn't think anything of her ability to sing beautifully because she only sings in the shower or the car. No wonder so many of us feel we're bigger than our lives, which is how Josie felt. We haven't found a place yet for all of our talents.

Have you ever wondered what would happen to a woman if she never gave birth to the baby she was carrying? It would kill her. In some way a part of us is dying because of all the special talents we carry inside us that we do nothing with.

"So I kept going to church a lot," Josie continued. "Frankly, I think a lot of people do who are going through tough times in their lives. But I started feeling there was something more there for me than just spiritual comfort food. I talked to my priest about it when I got over my embarrassment that I would sound like I was bragging. I was amazed when my priest told me that he'd always thought I was especially close to God. Then he said, 'There are many vocations in the Church—I know you have a talent for some of them. More than most of us.' That just blew me away. And then it hit me. No one had ever before praised me for having a talent for anything.

"When Father Boylan told me that, I kept asking myself what would I have a talent for besides just being happy sitting in church? Because they're not going to pay you for that. But Father Boylan had primed the pump for me. If I had some special talent, it couldn't have been completely invisible.

"So I started rethinking my time at the restaurant and—this is going to sound funny—but I was a really good teacher with the cooks and the waitstaff. I'd come out into the dining room a lot and schmooze: What I was really doing was teaching the customers about Italian food. People liked that. It's funny now looking back on my restaurant and thinking that the part I was best at was teaching."

"Okay," I said to Josie. "Everything happens for a reason. How can discovering you're a natural-born teacher be the meaning of losing your restaurant?"

"The truth is that I didn't really like the nuts and bolts of running a restaurant. I went into it because I wanted to be . . . really because I wanted to have my name on the sign and, when people came in, I was the queen. It's a lot of fun being *the fabulous Josie*. But what do you do with a talent? I sensed I had this talent for teaching, but I knew restaurants. So after . . . I was going to say after I was depressed, but I think this helped me get out of my depression, I came up with a vision of what a restaurant should be, a fun place for everyone, and I started marketing myself as a restaurant consultant, which meant I was really just a teacher. That actually went well because I had so many friends in the business.

"But there was still a sense that I also had a talent for God. Whatever talent I had there, I didn't want to let it rest. So I decided to talk to a variety of charities and to the missionary branches of some religious orders. My spirituality convinced me that I somehow had a vocation here somewhere, and that if I just stayed with it, I'd find that vocation.

"Now guess what? It turned out that one religious order does a lot of work with young people who've gotten in trouble and helps them by teaching them a trade. I signed on as a lay member of this order. I now train young people to become chefs and run a restaurant. There's no real money in this, but for the first time in my life, I'm really happy. I feel I'm living the life I was meant to live."

Josie had done intuitively what all of us can do if we're shown the way. Maybe she was just lucky that her intuition paid off. Maybe it was more than luck, though. Maybe a deep belief that everything happens for a reason and a willingness to look everywhere for that reason can take some people very far, as it did Josie.

But, you might ask, a talent is a good thing—why would it take some big dislocation in our lives to reveal our own talent to us? You have to look at our histories. Many of us, like Josie, were discouraged from thinking we have talent. Many of us are afraid of our talents. What if you have a talent for music, for example—do you really want to take the risks involved with becoming a musician? For many of us it is life itself that sub-merges our talents.

Out from Under

Someone who would answer *yes* to almost all of the diagnostic questions in this chapter is my mother. Fate gave her the back of its hand when she was growing up. She had been given the message loud and clear that she had nothing special to offer life and life had nothing special to offer her, nothing beyond work, obedience, and death.

Maybe she never *would* have felt she had anything to offer if it hadn't been for the Holocaust. Hitler invaded Poland the year my mother turned sixteen. Everyone in her family was killed. But somehow my mother met and married a young cavalry officer. Soon he was killed, but he left my mother with a son, my half brother.

By the end of the war, six years later, my mother had a second husband, a stepdaughter, another child (me), and the beginning of a whole new sense of herself. Halfway around the world in Central Asia, my mother, who might never have left her tiny village in Poland, who might never have discovered that she was capable of more than wiping a nose and washing a dish, found that she was an excellent businesswoman when she had to figure out ways to support her family. And she loved the world of business.

This is exactly like Robinson Crusoe's experience. Washed up on the shores of some disaster, we find some wonderful resource within us.

I want to make sure you don't misunderstand what I'm saying

here. It's true that I'm saying that discovering a hidden talent was a reason for my mother's going through what she did. That personal discovery did give meaning to the terrible losses in her life. But I'm not talking about one thing justifying another. I don't think 6 *billion* personal discoveries make up for even one death, much less the 6 million deaths of the Holocaust.

But this isn't about one thing making up for another. This is about, okay, the terrible thing *happened*, but it's happened, it's over, and now here you are with that loss. *Will it be a total loss, or will you be able to see that something valuable and meaningful can come from it?*

Discovering a hidden talent is actually a very big deal. It can save your life, as it did for my mother. It can save your emotional life, giving you the hope and energy to go on, as it did for Josie. It can save the life of the real you, the part of you that's special.

But how do you identify your talent if all you know, based on answering the diagnostic questions in this chapter, is that uncovering your talent is the reason you've gone through what you did?

Thinking Big

We have too small an idea of what talents are or of which talents are most important. If I tell you that someone's very talented, what's the first thought that comes into your head? Probably something artistic: singing, painting, writing, dancing. Maybe you think of something athletic. Maybe you think of math or handicrafts.

But we've already seen with Josie that the concept of talent can be taken much further. She turned out to have a talent for religion. The real truth is that anything that's important in life is something some people have a talent for. It's important to be happy, for example. My research (and that of many others) has shown that indeed some people have a talent for happiness.

And why not? What does the word *talent* mean anyway? It means that in some miraculous way you just "know" things without having to learn them. If you do learn, you learn much faster than other people and get much farther. Why can't a person have talent in this sense for any aspect of life you can imagine?

And then why wouldn't some huge event in your life come along to help you develop your hidden talent for, say, patience? Remember Doug, the guy whose son had gotten into trouble with drugs and disappeared? What do you think happens to people when someone they love has disappeared and they can't find him and all they can do is wait and hope? Here's what Doug said to me: "I never thought I was a patient guy. I run a business—how many guys like me are patient? But I think it's really hurt me, not acting patient. It hurt my marriage and my relationship with my son. I think it's hurt me in business, too. You need patience to have long-term goals. But I hadn't had any plan, for the firm or for how I'm going to develop clients or anything. But I think through all this I really have been discovering how patient I can be.

"Part of it is just my telling myself that patience is the virtue I need now. Suppose Dougie comes back? Am I going to blow it all by being impatient with him for wherever he's at? I thought a lot about what kind of father I'd been and how I wished I'd been more patient with Dougie. I can't exercise my patience with him now, though, but I can at work.

"At the shop—that's what we call the agency—I'm like everyone's dad a little bit. And I've really become much more patient. If someone has an idea or a point to make and they're not getting it over all that well, I give them a chance to get at what they want to say. It's been good, too. People talk more and some good ideas come out that I wouldn't have heard if I hadn't been so patient. If people are struggling with a project, I put my energy into helping them instead of yelling at them. They may not get it done as fast as I'd hoped, but it's usually a lot better than if they were just finishing up quickly because they didn't want to deal with my impatience."

Caught in his time bubble of hope and waiting, Doug made a simple decision: to be a more loving, more forgiving, more *patient* person everywhere in his life. He even changed how he dealt with his ex-wife.

Doug's new approach had a surprising impact on his business. A more patient approach to people extended to how he viewed the consumers he targeted with his ads. His ads became more human, warmer, sweeter, funnier, and they did a much better job of connecting with people. For the very first time Doug started winning awards for his ads. This brought his agency to clients' attention and brought him new business.

And Doug heard from his son about a year ago! It turns out the kid had gone to L.A. with nothing more in his head than the fact that there were drugs out there. But there was also an entertainment industry. He went through a period when things were terrible. He'd been beaten up, homeless, thrown into jail, and had to do things to hustle for money he would never tell his father about.

But he had an instinct that he could turn things around (was this a talent for patience with himself?—maybe buried treasure runs in families) and that he shouldn't contact his father until he was back on his feet. Dougie denied himself the help he needed to save his father from the burden of seeing how far his son had fallen.

And he did turn things around. When he called his father he was living in a halfway house connected to a drug rehab center. He'd just started work as a production assistant for a company that filmed commercials. He was incredibly proud of the fact that he'd launched himself into something connected to his father's business all by himself. Doug has flown out to L.A. to see his son several times. They talk on the phone a few times a week. Doug is now welcome in his son's life.

Seeing Your Specialness

How can other people make their own version of the journey Monica, Josie, and Doug made? The first step of this journey happened when they saw that the reason they went through some challenging event in their lives was to help them discover a hidden talent. The next step was seeing what that talent is. And the final step was using that knowledge to make their lives better.

Here's how you can make this journey yourself.

First, answer the diagnostic questions. You've probably done that, so you probably already know whether the meaning of what happened to you was to help you find a buried talent.

But what is that talent? You might just *see* what your talent is, the way Doug did. After all, when I talked to people, they didn't say the reason they suffered a tough break was "to discover a talent." They just said, "I realized how good I was at . . . " But they never saw it as a result of merely sitting at home stewing in their own juices. They saw it as a result of throwing themselves into the new life that appeared to them after the tough break. It was in the new things they did in that new life that they saw their hidden talent.

If you see it, then understand what a big deal it is. It's not just a mint on your pillow. It's the meaning of what happened to you.

But if you haven't seen it yet, *here's the next step.* I've talked about these undiscovered talents as buried treasure. But the truth is that treasure like this is never completely buried. Some glimpse of it has already been revealed to you. It's not really a problem of discovering a hidden talent. It's more a problem of realizing what it is that you've already discovered. To do that you have to bring it to your own awareness.

One technique is this: You've always suspected there was something special about you. So say what it is, whatever comes into your head. Don't look for just one thing. Look for a minimum of ten things. Write down the longest list you can think of. That way you're bound to hit on something that's really a buried treasure.

Here's another technique: We've all had moments in our lives when we've *shone*. It was a shining moment for you when you did something special or in a special way, when you were wonderful, if only for a moment. Maybe no one saw it, but you felt a kind of shining inside yourself. Each of these ways you've shone is a way you're special.

For example, maybe you've noticed that when your friends have problems they come to you and you're often able to be amazingly helpful. You wouldn't want to brag, but to be honest you know that these are moments when you shine. That's a marker of a way you're special.

Or maybe you have one of those kits at home with fifty different-colored felt-tipped markers and you make these crazy pictures with them. Who knows if it's good art? But it feels wonderful to do it and it's wonderful to look at what you've done. You know you feel like you're shining with these, so you know that's a way you're special.

Or maybe you look back and realize that over and over you've walked into messy situations that have overwhelmed other people and somehow you've been able to quickly organize them: a messy checkbook, a messy kitchen, a messy business. Whatever the mess is in your case, your memory of having shone has to do with transforming these messes into order. This is a way you're special.

Be clear about one thing: Sensing the ways you're special has nothing to do with winning praise or approval from anyone else. *You* know how you're special. You're the judge of this. Maybe you've written a lot of poems and no one's ever wanted to publish them. But instead of thinking they're crap, you keep looking at them and they make you happy because they shine with something special that comes from you. Then you should believe and trust that there are people out there who will recognize your talent.

You also need to look carefully at the bad thing that happened to you to see if somehow that directly revealed a talent you might not have believed in otherwise. Take Linda. In her mid-thirties she started finding that she was tired all the time, dragging herself through her days, always needing to nap. Even when she ate healthfully and had plenty of sleep she was exhausted. She made the rounds of doctors, who first said it was all in her head. Eventually Linda was diagnosed with a medical condition that was uncommon but still affected a lot of people.

Linda responded to all of this in a special way. Rather than just being another victim of the medical system, Linda did a ton of research online and in medical libraries and then went still further by starting support groups and even a website that serves as a switchboard of information for other people with this problem.

Physically Linda is still not 100 percent. And things were very bad for a long time. But in her direct response to her illness Linda uncovered capabilities that gave her a new life.

Now for the third step. If you've been fortunate enough to discover that the meaning of what happened to you is that you have something far more to offer than you ever imagined, *you have to offer it.* Bring it out of yourself and into the world. This isn't easy. It takes trial and error. You might find obstacles to discovering how an artistic talent can best be expressed, for example. Just remember that certainty you felt inside about how you were special. That's real. You have to let it see the light by doing something with it. And don't give up until you do.

Real Life, Real Love

———— ◆•◆ ————

I don't know what it's like in your town, but here in Boston if you use a hundred-dollar bill to pay for your groceries, they examine it twelve ways from Sunday to make sure it's real. And why not? They've probably been burned a lot by counterfeit bills.

There's also a lot of counterfeit love going around these days. There are relationships where the word *love* is used to paper over selfishness, distance, and anger. There are women who say, "But I love him," as a way of trapping themselves in a marriage that gives them much more pain than pleasure. There are men who want to find love but don't want to give it.

Anyone can be in a relationship. Anyone can justify any behavior in the name of love. But just the way a counterfeit bill is worthless, just the way food with empty calories provides no nutrition, love that's not real can never be satisfying.

Time to Answer Your Wake-Up Call

Sometimes we need to have our lives turned upside down to make us see we've been putting up with counterfeit love. Something huge has to happen in our lives to show us there's an alternative. We need a crisis to shake us out of our laziness, blindness, and fear. And that's good because deep down we're hungry for the real thing, and we need it, even if we don't seem to realize it yet.

Oh, and by the way, this wake-up call may not be an event that directly has anything to do with love, like a relationship that blew up in your face. It could be a car accident, a spell of unemployment, anything.

Wouldn't it be wonderful to know that you've already had that wake-up call and that it's given you everything you need to bring real, lasting, high-quality love into your life? Maybe you've failed to realize how much love you have to give. Maybe you've been too willing to put up with relationships that can never give you genuine, healthy love. Maybe you've been afraid to commit to or to work at the love you've found in your life.

And now there's the possibility that all this can change.

Just answer the following diagnostic questions:

- Do you feel that you've made more than your share of mistakes when it comes to love?
- Are you afraid you're unlovable?
- Have you too often felt that you haven't found real love? (You may have had plenty of relationships, but you haven't found the kind of love you need in those relationships.)
- Have you too often felt lonely in your life?

- Have you ever lost a great relationship filled with the possibility of love because you didn't value it, nurture it, give time and your best self to it?
- Is it usually hard for you to be yourself in your relationships?

If you answered *yes* to four or more of these questions, the reason you went through what you did was to learn an important lesson about bringing real love into your life.

Is that you? It's a lot of us these days. And that's primarily because habit, fear of being alone, worship of image, low self-esteem, and a host of other factors would make it hard for some people to recognize real love if it grabbed them by the heart.

What Is Real Love?

I spent several years studying love leading up to my book *Women & Love*, a study of women's search for real love in their lives and what they need to be successful in this search.

In the process I found *the elements of real love*, based on the way men and women define real love when you get them to open up about their hopes and disappointments, when they can see the mistakes they've made in the past and understand what they need and want to do differently in the future:

- Real love is not just how you feel about your partner. It's much more how your partner makes you feel about yourself.
- Real love is not about losing yourself in your partner. It's about becoming true to yourself with your partner.
- Real love is not about how great your partner is. It's about how great you can become alongside your partner.

- Real love is not just about how much you love your partner. It's about how your partner helps you love yourself.

- Real love is not just about your partner finding room in his or her heart for you. It's about your partner finding room in his or her life for your energy, drive, ambition, passions, interests, and needs.

- Real love is not just based on how good your partner is "deep down." It's based on how much you actually experience your partner's goodness as you live your life together.

- Real love is not based on how your partner makes you hungry to be with him or her. It's based on how much your partner makes you feel at home when you are with each other.

- Real love is not about the love you say you share. It's about the life you really do share, fully, equally, deeply.

- Real love is about treating your partner the way you'd want to be treated.

- Real love is about falling in *like*.

I realize that these signs of real love constitute a pretty high standard. Most of us fall short of this standard a lot of the time in our relationships. But some of us aren't even close. Then something happens, and it turns out that the reason it did was to give us what we need to find real love like this.

That's what happened to me.

The Battle for Love

In the middle of war-torn Europe, men and women were hungry for safety and connection. That's what brought my mother and father together, not love. The same turbulent world that brought them together created the stresses that drove them apart. My parents divorced just before I turned four. After their divorce my mother came to America and we settled in New York. I begged her to get me a new father. I desperately wanted the love I'd thought there'd be if my mother got married and we had a family again.

I was six when she announced out of the clear blue sky that I had a new father. She'd been a single woman with two young children. A refugee. A survivor. The man she married was much older and was looking for someone to take care of him and help him with his little business. To say the least, this was not a love match.

It was more like an endless emotional boxing match. From the very beginning they seemed to hate each other and do nothing but yell at each other. Today as a professional who's worked with thousands of couples, I can see that they simply had a terrible relationship and should never have been together.

I spent much of my childhood watching them fight and dreaming about the possibility of real love. Once you start thinking about real love, it raises a thousand questions. You start examining every bill to see if it's counterfeit. And so I was never even sure my mother loved *me*. She took very good care of my physical needs. I was never abused. But the warmth and acceptance you expect from a mother were missing.

I can't possibly criticize this woman who'd been through hell and who had saved my life with her struggle to keep us alive. I know she did her best. But she had little to work with. I don't think she'd ever gotten any real affection herself. What she knew about affection was what you'd know if, like her, you were the oldest of seven brothers and sisters, your parents were poor Jewish peasant farmers on someone else's land, and you had to take care of everyone else and no one took care of you. And then when you were nine years old you were shipped off to be a kind of servant in some other family and your first and only love was killed before you ever really got to know him, before you turned seventeen. And all the other men you'd known had treated you badly.

Watching my mother and stepfather fight and feeling my own hunger for love—this would definitely qualify as a bad event in my life. And it was one of the things about which I asked, "How could something like this possibly have any meaning?"

I now know it did have positive meaning, and real value for me. Just look at what happened as a result of it. I got married at twenty and I'm still married to the same man. It hasn't always been easy, but keeping our love healthy has always been a top priority for me.

It feels clear to me that the reason I was deprived of an atmosphere of love when I was growing up was so I could see how important love is—for me, for all of us. You might think, *Who doesn't know that?* Well, it was not so obvious to someone like me. I like to be alone. I like to work hard. I don't like distractions. I'm quirky. I could so easily never have found anyone to love. I could so easily have ruined all of my relationships by making them low priorities. But the lesson I learned growing up made it possible for me to have love in my life—I was committed to doing whatever was necessary to find real love and keep it healthy.

So my experience with love growing up had meaning for me not because of the nature of that experience but because of my own nature. Maybe as soon as I was born the people who run Cosmic Kindergarten took one look at me and knew exactly the kind of lesson someone like me would need to learn. I'm not saying it does work like this. But I am saying that it sure seems as though it works like this.

Understanding the true importance of love is one of the meanings of the events in my life. Frankly, I was a little taken aback when I first saw this. *Moi?!* I was happily married. I was a couples therapist. I'd written three books about relationships. But pride has no place in Cosmic Kindergarten. Nothing kills the possibility of learning as thoroughly as pride, because pride makes it impossible for you to see that there's anything you could learn. When I let go of my pride I saw that for me the need to relearn the lessons of love was endless.

So when we see the lessons Cosmic Kindergarten has designed for us to learn, we should feel good about it. If these lessons have to do with finding real love, that just means your future is going to be much better than your past.

Lessons Everywhere

Life always makes things happen to people to show them the true importance of love. The lessons can come from anywhere. I knew a beautiful actress who discovered she was infertile. When Susan's then-boyfriend found out, he dumped her. It was a terribly painful rejection. For a long time she couldn't stop feeling that she was barren, worthless, not a real woman, that no one would possibly want her.

But everything happens for a reason. Susan had been plagued for years with the wrong guys liking her for the wrong reasons. Her "problem" was that she was not only great looking but she had a sweet, friendly disposition. A guy would know her for two seconds and think she was incredibly easy, not in the sense that she'd go to bed with him but in the sense that this was a relationship that would give him a lot and require very little from him. In other words, Susan kept attracting shallow, selfish, self-centered men.

Now she'd have to tell potential boyfriends about her infertility. At first this seemed like a terrible cross to bear. But it was actually a gift. Sure, lots of guys would bail out when they heard her news. But they were exactly the kinds of guys who'd been plaguing Susan. Some guys, though, would stick around. They were the guys who felt, *Hey, I never expected it would be easy, but you're worth it.* These were guys who were willing to pay the price of admission.

And this gave Susan enormous help in understanding the true importance of love. Before this, her taste in men had been pretty superficial: arm candy, guys she could use to impress her girlfriends—in other words, men who almost guaranteed that lasting love would come last in a relationship with Susan. Now she was forced to be more discriminating, to focus more on what was most important in love, since she wasn't going to have anything more to do with guys who couldn't appreciate what was most important about love to her.

Now you might wonder if there's anyone who needs help understanding the true importance of love. Don't we all worship at the altar of love?

Maybe we serve at that altar, but it's mostly lip service. We talk about how important love is but then we allow a lot of other priorities to creep in. The result is that if you look at our lives as they actually are, there's too often little real love in them, love that truly brings us close, love that makes us feel good about ourselves and brings out the best in us, love that's based on truly liking and respecting the other person.

No wonder we so often need to learn a lesson about love. Let's figure out what that lesson is in your case.

"What I Wish I'd Done Differently"

The lesson is a wake-up call, driving home the idea that you need to take love a lot more seriously and really shows that you should insist on the highest-quality love. If you answered *yes* to four or more of the diagnostic questions in this chapter, consider yourself woken up. Now you know—nothing less than true love for you from now on.

This is an extremely valuable lesson. Most people say that they know the value of love but that having a successful relationship is a complex and mysterious process. The opposite is true. I see this in my work every day. Most people *have* a lot of information about how to make their relationships satisfying. But they don't implement this information because they don't give the *highest priority* to the things that ensure real love. They know what to do but they don't do it.

Al was a patient of mine. Over time I discovered that he was a genuinely good person. He would never deliberately hurt anyone. But here's what happened at his wedding. After the service and the reception at the country club, he was in a great mood. Why not? He'd just married the most beautiful, wonderful woman in the world. He sat out on the lawn with his buddies smoking cigars, basking in his happiness. As time passed, his new bride waited for him inside. She'd arranged with Al that as a romantic ritual he'd come in at around 10:00 P.M. and help her take off her wedding gown. But Al never came. He'd forgotten. But his bride never forgot how she had to ask her mother to help her out of her gown and how disappointed she felt waiting for him. Al knew the right thing to do. He just didn't make it his highest priority.

No wonder we need a wake-up call. Just like Al, in one way or another we're always missing opportunities in our relationships.

Custom-Tailored Love Lessons

The event in your life has also offered you a valuable pointer about exactly what you need to do to work harder or smarter to bring real love into your life. What is that pointer in your case?

Here's how to "read" one of these events of your life to see what you need to find true love. Something happens to you that's a wake-up call about the quality of love in your life. (You know that because of your answers to the diagnostic questions in this chapter.) It could be any kind of event whatsoever, often having nothing to do with love.

Ask yourself what you wish you'd done differently in that event. You'll come up with something like *If only I'd paid more attention to what I really needed,* or *If only I'd been more honest about who I really am.*

Now you have to take that *if only* and point it toward the

future. Instead of thinking about what you wish you'd done differently in the past, think about how you can do things differently in the future. *From now on in my relationship I'm going to pay more attention to what I really need and make sure my important needs get met,* or *From now on in all my relationships I'm going to be more honest about who I really am even if I find that a little scary.*

You can't fix the past, but you can fix your life if you do in the future what you wish you'd done in the past.

Man Bonked on Head by Falling Flowerpot

Here's an example of how Cosmic Kindergarten teaches us lessons about love. Louis, a guy I talked to in my research on the meaning of the events in our lives, had been walking up Park Avenue in New York. A plant in a small plastic flowerpot fell out of a window, bonked him on the head, knocked him out, and gave him a concussion. If it had been something heavier or had fallen out of a higher window, it would've killed him.

As Louis answered the diagnostic questions here it became clear that the meaning of what happened had something to do with giving him what he needed to find real love. But what was the specific lesson he needed to learn? And how do you figure out that lesson when you've been hit on the head with a plastic flowerpot?

I asked Louis what he wished he'd done differently around this experience. He said, "It's funny you asked. There's nothing I could've done differently. I was just walking down the street. But here's the thing: When I woke up from being knocked out and finally understood what had happened, the first thing I thought was that I could've been killed so easily. And *then* I thought, *I wish I'd been nicer to my wife.* We're so mean to the people we care about sometimes because we think we're going to live forever and so we have all the time in the world to patch things up. But of course we don't. If I can die at any minute, then my mean, selfish words can easily be the very last things my wife is going to remember about me."

Louis's *if only* was *If only I'd been nicer to my wife.* It's easy to translate that into what he needs to do differently in the future for the love in his life to be real: Be nicer to his wife. It's obvious.

The meaning of an event in your life doesn't come from the event. It comes from you and the lessons you're needing to learn. But once you know, by answering the diagnostic questions, that the meaning for you has to do with getting what you need to find true love, you're going to want to know what lesson you got. And this is where you can turn to the event, whatever it is.

> Just ask yourself: *What mistakes or omissions in my life does this event point to or remind me of? What do I wish I'd done differently while I was going through it?* Your answers will show you what you need to do so you can have a higher quality of love in your life.

This is what Louis did. If he can do it about a flowerpot falling on his head, we can do it about anything.

The Most Important Lesson

Now you know how to read a particular event in your life, the one whose meaning you were looking for, to see what to do to find real love. This makes it easy to see the specific lessons

Cosmic Kindergarten was trying to teach you. Of course, everyone learns a slightly different lesson. Still, there's one lesson that came up for so many people and came through so loud and clear that I'll save you the trouble of looking for it. If for some reason you just can't figure out what you wish you'd done differently in the past so you can apply it to your future relationships, apply this lesson and you won't go wrong:

Love is richest, most genuine, and most long lasting when you focus on being yourself and doing everything you can to make it possible for the other person to be him- or herself.

The truth about who you are and what you need is going to come out anyway. The sooner it comes out, the sooner you can get on a path where you'll find real love.

This is what Jennifer discovered. When I first talked to her she was forty-four, outdoorsy-looking from the waist down in hiking boots and jeans, like someone who liked to hike in the mountains. But from the waist up she wore a mustard-yellow sweater and pearls.

Five years earlier her husband had been killed returning from a business trip when his airliner crashed on takeoff. She was still in mourning. As we talked, she gave me the impression that they'd been one of those golden couples, happy together and in love, with everything to look forward to. In one moment, her dreams and her future were smashed. All she could do was get on with the business of raising her son.

But on some level she'd never been able to get back in the swim of life. The sheer senselessness of her husband's death left Jennifer feeling utterly vulnerable. If everything happened for no good reason whatsoever, she said, then nothing made any sense. Why plan? Why have hope?

I could see what was at stake for her. Would she spend her life emotionally crippled by what had happened or would she find a way to make peace with it and finally be able to embrace whatever life she was meant to live? This would make all the difference between being alone for the rest of her life and finding true love again, between feeling that she was stuck in limbo and feeling like herself again.

"Don't get me wrong," Jennifer said. "I think I'm a positive person. I love life and I don't feel guilty about being happy. It's just that . . . you know, when Edward was killed I was lost in darkness and then things started getting lighter and I thought I'd get all the way back to brightness. But I stayed stuck at dark gray. That's why I came to see you: to find the light again."

As we talked I had the sense that everything hadn't been perfect in Jennifer and Edward's relationship. This was a sign that there were things Jennifer needed to learn. Cosmic Kindergarten can be a very hard-nosed school. It will keep holding you back until you learn the lesson you're needing to learn. This is why many of us are stuck in our lives. Learn, already! Then you'll be able to move on.

Before long Jennifer opened up to me. "When my husband died I had all these regrets. God, every time I'd gotten mad at him, every time he'd wanted to make love and I'd put him off for some stupid reason—I regretted everything. But that's just stuff everyone does. I also started thinking more deeply about my marriage and I started having this whole new regret that even now I have trouble forgiving myself for—that I wasn't really myself with Edward. Most of the time I just tried to be the kind of person he wanted me to be. Then sometimes I'd get into a mood and I'd act mean. But neither of those people were really me. I think I'm a dreamier, goofier, more romantic person than I let him see. I like being outdoors a lot more. Stuff like that.

"And the reason this still makes me so sad"—tears started flowing down Jennifer's cheeks—"is that . . . were we ever really married? Did he ever really love me if he never knew the real me?"

"So you regret the fact that you didn't let him see the real you. Okay. Now what are you going to do differently next time?" I asked.

"What do you mean next time? There is no next time."

"You see, that's why you're stuck. You can't even imagine a next time because you haven't let in the lesson you need to learn. You're caught in a paradox. The bigger the lesson you're needing to learn, the more you think it somehow invalidates your marriage to Edward—at least that's what you're afraid of—and the less you want to learn that lesson. But you don't need to worry about invalidating your marriage. Your genuine grief is all the validation your marriage needs. Now you need to think about moving forward. But that's not going to be possible until you let in the lesson that's standing there right in front of your eyes. You've already said what it is."

"You're right. I haven't really dared to imagine the possibility of my being myself in a relationship. Maybe I've been afraid. What a scary thought—to just be who I am."

That was it. For many people this is the scariest question

they can imagine: Will I still be loved if I show my real self? But if you show who you really are and you're rejected, it hurts, yes, but at least you're spared a lifetime of hiding. If you show who you are and you're loved, then you know you're really loved, and it's the only way to feel that you're really loved.

That's why a radical decision to be yourself comes up so often for people who have gone through hell—to wake them up to the importance of finding real love. It's hard, it's risky, but if you don't show who you really are, you'll never feel really loved and you'll never be able to give the love you're capable of giving.

If you just think about it a moment, this makes an awful lot of sense. What in the world is Cosmic Kindergarten for if it's not about helping you become your best, most authentic self? And where in the world is it more important for this to happen than in the land of love?

Solid Like a Rock

———◆·◆·◆———

"What doesn't kill you makes you stronger." We're used to the idea that the difficulties of life make us stronger. There's just one problem with this: If I tell you that you've gone through some serious difficulty so you can become stronger, you're going to want to know stronger *how?*

When I talked to people who'd finally understood that the true reason why something had happened to them was to help them become stronger, they all said that the reason was to make them stronger in a very specific way. Their loss or ordeal not only gave them a specific strength, it gave them just the strength they were needing to take the next step in their lives.

Maybe something happened to test their patience. But it taught them how to be patient, and that was perfect because they were about to become new parents.

Maybe something happened that made them regret terribly that they hadn't listened to themselves. But that made them see how essential it is for them to listen to themselves whenever they make a decision, and that was just what they needed to deal with at a time of change in their lives.

Maybe they had a heart disease or a cancer scare. But that forced them to start exercising, eating better, and generally taking good care of their bodies, and that was just what they needed going into middle age.

"Why Shouldn't Your Life Be Filled with Gifts?"

Three weeks after graduating from college, Sandi married the guy she'd been dating for the past four years. Ten years later she realized she'd spent all that time with a boring guy she didn't love and who didn't make her happy. She knew her relationship was over, and yet she couldn't end it.

What held Sandi back was her sense of the meaninglessness of it all. Could she really have thrown away her twenties by being with the wrong guy? Sandi felt she had to stay in the relationship just to avoid the sense that she'd wasted all those years for no good reason.

That's how it is for many of us. Until we find a way to tap into the meaning of the events in our lives, we can't trust ourselves or our futures, and so we're paralyzed.

Sandi had talked to her friends endlessly about her marriage. When she said there was nothing there for her, they encouraged her to leave. When she said she hated the thought that it was all such a waste, they said maybe she should stick around and try to make it work. Sandi felt utterly confused.

Finally, Sandi decided to talk to her grandmother about her dilemma. This was a big step because her grandmother was the family matriarch. She'd come alone to the United States from China in her early twenties. She'd built a small but successful wholesale business importing Chinese handicrafts for sale to gift shops. Sandi remembered working as a child in her grandmother's showroom setting up displays, and even when she'd knocked over a carefully arranged pile of merchandise her grandmother had never gotten mad at her.

Sandi's grandmother was similarly unperturbed when Sandi told her about her iffy marriage. She got right to the point. "You should be happy. Why live if you can't be happy, right? And you're a beautiful girl. You can easily find someone who will make you happy. But I know why you can't make yourself leave your husband. You think, *What a waste, all those years,* and you don't want to think that. But I don't think those years were a waste. I think they were a gift.

"I remember when you were in high school and college. No self-confidence. That's what I saw. When you were nineteen it was like you were nine. I remember thinking, *Okay, it's going to take my little Sandi a long time to become a woman who feels strong enough to stand on her own two feet.* And now here you are and you think your marriage was such a waste and so meaningless. Why are you so sure it was meaningless? What if it was a gift for you, just the gift you were needing?" And her grandmother made a sweeping gesture as if to say, *Why, just look at all the gifts that fill this room—why shouldn't your life be filled with gifts?*

"How was it a gift for me," Sandi asked, "to throw away my twenties with a husband who wasn't right for me? And there are no children and we have no future?"

"You're so closed minded," her grandmother said. "So sad for someone so young. But suppose you'd been saved from this hell. Suppose that little nine-year-old girl in a nineteen-year-old woman's body, a woman with no self-confidence, had spent all those years going out with different boys. I was a young woman. I know what it's like. When you have no confidence, men can take all your energy. You were such a scared little girl, and then you would've had your heart broken by all these different boyfriends. Where would your self-confidence have been then?

"But you were very smart even though you think you were stupid. You said, *Okay, if I'm so insecure, let me buy myself some time.* How smart you were. You got yourself married. And that made you free of all the worry and insecurity you would've had to face as a single woman. What have you spent the last ten years doing? I'm very proud of you. You're very successful at your work. You concentrated on your work because you were free and because you were married. Your marriage gave you the strength you needed to be successful at work. That gave you the foundation you needed—the confidence you've gotten from being successful at work has given you the strength you need to seek the right man. See? Aren't you a smart girl?"

For the first time Sandi felt that she could see past the cliché when all her friends had said, "Everything happens for a reason." It wasn't a cliché if there really was a reason. And her grandmother had shown Sandi the reason.

Why hadn't she been able to see it for herself? Like many of us, Sandi was trapped by thinking that bad events only have negative meanings. She'd looked at something bad that had happened to her like it was a bad tree that can only bring forth bad fruit. But the events in our lives that we're trying to make sense of are not the tree. The tree is our lives themselves. And over and over I've seen that our lives were designed to bring forth good fruit.

A Firmer Foundation

The best way to know that the events of our lives are bringing forth good fruit is to look at what we need. Sandi needed the opportunity and time to strengthen her self-confidence. Maybe there's some specific way you've needed to become stronger, and maybe your life has already given it to you.

Do you fall into this category? Here's how you can tell for sure. Answer the following diagnostic questions:

- Have you had more than your share of loss in your life?
- Has low self-esteem been an issue for you?
- Do you have trouble identifying things in your life that can't be taken away from you?
- Has it been your experience that most things in life are impermanent—relationships, friends, jobs, and so on?
- Do you feel you're under serious threat of losing what you have?
- Are you hungry to have something in your life that you're really good at?
- Have you felt there's something important missing at your core?

+ Do you feel that your ability to move forward into your future is blocked?

A *yes* answer to four or more of these questions reveals that there is a reason for what happened to you, and it's to help you become stronger in some specific way. And this is true no matter what the event was, because the meaning of an event comes from who you are and what you need, not from the event itself.

How I can say that these questions determine whether the meaning of some event is to give you a way to become stronger? I've talked to many people who discovered that becoming stronger was the meaning of what happened to them. And they, too, would have answered *yes* to four or more of the above questions.

Most people are stronger than they think. We get scared, overwhelmed, and sad, and all these emotions make us think we're weak. Occasionally they even knock us flat on our back. But then we recover, we cope, and we triumph.

Don't let your feelings make you think you're weaker than you are. Yet many of us still need to become strengthened. Here's why.

A Foundation Is a Springboard

We need to become stronger because we need more of a foundation. A foundation gives you a basis for something else above and beyond it, just as the concrete foundation under your house is the basis for your house. Certain foundational tennis skills are the basis of your tennis game. Having a good foundation in people skills is part of the basis for a successful career in business. So you may have needed to have your foundation strengthened in a certain way because you needed a basis for doing something brand-new, or because you'd never had a basis for doing something that's very important to you.

And that's why things happen to us sometimes—to give us a special strength that makes a new future possible.

Growing up is a lifelong process for everyone. I know people in their eighties and nineties who are still picking up missing pieces in their development. And fortunately, over and over again life comes to your aid just when you need it. When Sandi, for example, became an adult, her self-confidence was still a work in progress. Cosmic Kindergarten came to her aid. It made it possible for Sandi to build up her confidence at work, and this gave her just enough of an overall sense of confidence to be able to go forward and find the kind of relationship she wanted.

When you think of all the things you're trying to do now and all the things that may be important for you to do in the future, it takes a pretty broad foundation to support all of that. So it's not surprising that there'd be a part of your foundation that needs strengthening. What part? Any part.

It might be something incredibly specific. For example, your father was transferred to Paris when you were a teenager and you spent four miserable years, your precious high school years, going to school in France. *Quelle dommage!* But everything happens for a reason. You learned French really well. That might not seem like a big deal, foundationwise. But somehow it got you into a really good college and opened the door to a career in international law, which was exciting and suited you perfectly.

It might be putting your life on a more solid footing. Joe's company transferred him to a facility in an isolated rural environment. For six years he thought he'd go out of his mind because there was nothing to do. "Why am I being punished like this?" he asked himself over and over. But everything happens for a reason, and it turns out that six years of nothing to do is six years of no way to spend your money. For the first time in his life, Joe was able to save a considerable amount of money, giving him a financial foundation he'd never had before.

It might be developing an inner strength. One woman I know grew up with a father who drank, and then had to watch her older brothers get into trouble as they became heavy drinkers. She lived for years with all that misery and suffering. But everything happens for a reason. She saw that people need a foundation of happiness under them, and that, in fact, happiness is a choice. She saw the men in her life choosing to be miserable. And that gave her an amazing strength: It made it possible for her to choose to be happy, a choice she continued to make every single day from that point on.

Foundational strengths are the seeds of new futures. But what future? How do you discover that what happened to you strengthened you in a way that gives you a new future?

Something That Can Never Be Taken from You

Adam, twenty-nine, was a patient of mine. He was a quiet, pleasant, compact, thoughtful man just beginning a career as an art historian at a major university. He came to see me because he was going through a crisis that took him unaware.

I liked him immediately. He'd recently married a woman he loved very much and with whom he was looking forward to building a family. But after their wedding he found himself starting to get depressed and unaccountably resisting the idea of their having children.

"Why is this happening to me?" he asked me. This goes on all the time in my work with people—they wake up one day to find themselves tied in a knot and they come to me to figure out how everything got so knotted and what they can do about it.

We take it for granted that everyone has a childhood of some sort. Adam missed most of his childhood because he was born with multiple congenital heart problems that were misdiagnosed and mistreated at an early stage. From the ages of five through eleven, Adam was a semi-invalid. He was unable to go to school or play outdoors with other children. It was as if his life had a huge hole in it.

Like most kids, Adam eventually got used to the hand he'd been dealt growing up. Entering his new wife's family, however, reminded him of how much he'd missed. There were all the stories and home movies of his wife and her sisters playing actively as kids. As he put it, "The more time I spent with my wife's family, the bluer I got. It's like I'd never realized how much I'd lost and I had to go through mourning all over again. But it was the kind of loss that seems permanent and unhealable. Every time I saw my wife's family I'd be reminded of what I'd never gotten." He paused. "And what I still need."

Adam tried to put it all in perspective for me. "I don't feel sorry for myself. But here's the thing. For me there's still this *mystery.* I compare my nonchildhood with my wife's wonderful childhood—can it mean nothing?"

"Why not try this?" I suggested. "What if we only *think* we don't know the reason why something happened to us, like your losing all those years growing up? What if deep down we do know and we show that we know by the way we live? Suppose we looked at what you're doing in your life now and said *that's* where you'll find the answer to the question 'What did I learn from all this?' When you see what you learned, you'll see the reason why you went through what you did."

"What did I learn?" Adam thought for a moment. "Sometimes I think I never outgrew the picture books I read when I was a little kid stuck in bed. By the time I was in college, I'd come to love painting. And I took this little introductory art history course and the woman who taught it *knew every painting that had ever been painted.* And how all the artists were influenced by other artists. And I thought, *Wow, that's what I want to do with my life.* You get to look at all these beautiful paintings, and you *know everything.* My colleagues really love art, too, but the fact that there's so much to know they find kind of annoying and overwhelming. To me that's what I love about it."

"Okay, so when you know everything about art history . . . well, so what?"

"I keep going back to my professors who knew everything. They're like a rock. They're so solid. If you have a theory, someone can prove your theory wrong. But if you know every image created by Raphael and Rembrandt and hundreds of painters no one's ever heard of—that can never be taken from you. Never." And the tears started rolling down Adam's cheeks.

"Now quickly say the first thing that comes into your mind. 'The reason I lost my childhood was . . . ' what?"

"The reason I lost my childhood was to teach me that I can lose almost anything, but there have to be some things that I can never lose, like really knowing something, and I'd better have as many of those things in my life as I can. So I'll still be strong in a way that can't be taken away from me." Suddenly he was silent. It hit him that he'd found what he'd been looking for.

"So that gives a very special meaning to the knowledge you've acquired, doesn't it?"

"It must be why I'm still so hungry to know everything about art. Every time I learn something I didn't know before, I feel safer and stronger."

"We're not done, Adam. Why you? I mean, what is it about you that would make this so important to you?"

"I was this skinny, short, dark little boy and I was very quiet. I did well with my schoolwork but I wasn't special. My worst fear was that I'd never be good at anything. It's like that was the big question, Was I going to be somebody in my parents' eyes or nothing? And that was very intimidating. I think the difference now is that I don't think about being special or wonderful. The pressure's off. There's just art, and it's beautiful and interesting and I love it. But I needed a solid foundation. Something like the dikes the Dutch built to hold back the sea. My foundation would hold back my sense of loss. It would be insurance against loss. You can't lose knowledge."

"So the reason you lost your childhood," I said, "was to learn how important it is to really know something. Because then you'd have a strength that could never be taken away from you. Yes?"

EVERYTHING HAPPENS FOR A REASON

"Yeah. I think that's what this gave me. And I think that if that hadn't happened, then maybe I'd have been one of those people who just want to be special. I know a lot of people like that in the art world and deep down they're in despair because they know they're not really very special. But if you know something or know how to do something—it could be knowing how to bake bread, anything—it's so real and solid you never have to worry about how special you are."

Connecting the Dots

If you're hungry to discover the meaning of some event in your life, remember that you've been in Cosmic Kindergarten for quite a while now. Maybe you've already found the meaning of this event and have made very good use of it, but, like Adam, you just don't realize it yet.

All you need to do is look at what you've got in your life right now that means the most to you. Connect the dots. There's some really tough event that happened a while back. . . . You know you were needing to become stronger in some way. . . . There's this wonderful thing in your life right now, even if it's just a possibility. Okay, then. Bad event . . . becoming stronger . . . wonderful life right now. Just connect the dots.

> *The bad event gave you the strength you needed in your foundation to make possible what's wonderful in your life right now.*

For example, one guy got laid off, was unemployed for six months, got a new job, got laid off again, and was unemployed for a year before he found decent work. This was a painful and scary period (the *bad event*). "Never again," he said. He then dedicated himself to going back to school and upgrading his skills (the *stronger foundation*). By doing this he actually created a meaning for what happened to him out of what he did in response to it. This happened almost twenty years ago, and this guy has never stopped working and growing (the *wonderful life* he made for himself).

But not everyone has an easy time connecting the dots. That's because not everyone can see what there is to connect the dots to. Everyone who answered *yes* to four or more of the questions here has become stronger in some important way. That's the meaning of what happened for them. But not everyone has built on this strength yet. Maybe that's why it was hard for you to connect the dots.

Is that you? By themselves foundations are sort of useless-looking, white-elephant kinds of things. There's no reason to have a foundation unless you build on it. "What if that's me?" I hear you asking. Well, don't panic. The important thing is strengthening your foundation. And if the meaning of what happened to you lies here, you have strengthened your foundation. You've taken all but the last step. But of course, as the man said who was running to hop on a ferry and fell in the water, it's the last step that gets you every time.

You're probably much closer than you think.

"If I Could Only Do This . . . "

I was interviewing a young woman, Lisa, who'd progressively lost almost all her hearing with little prospect that she'd get it back. We communicated by e-mail. Like most people who have a loss like this as an adult, Lisa was deeply discouraged. I asked Lisa the diagnostic questions in this chapter. She answered *yes* to all of them. And she found herself feeling uncomfortable—she couldn't see how she'd strengthened her foundation. And she was sure she hadn't done anything to build on it.

Here's what Lisa said: "In the weeks after I learned that I was going to go deaf, I started thinking, *Okay, I'm going to have to compensate for this, like the way Ray Charles compensated for being blind by being a really great singer and piano player.* You know, we cripples and gimps have to find our compensation. But how? I can't sing. But then I realized that's *it.* It doesn't have to be singing. The important thing is finding something I could do really well. Then as I was going through rehab I realized for the first time that I had the drive to be able to do something really well. So what do I do now? I want to do something really well. But I don't know what. How can this somehow be the meaning of what happened to me, to feel good and strong knowing that I want to do something really well but then not know what it is?"

"Why is it so important to you to do something really well?"

"That's not a hard question," Lisa said. "I want to feel good about myself. I want to accomplish something. I want something that can never be taken away from me."

"So ask yourself this: *What would you like to have in your life that can never be taken away from you?* You said that you really connected with the idea of some area of your life where you want to do something really well. Can you try to link those two thoughts: wanting to do something really well and wanting to have something that can never be taken from you?"

Lisa didn't answer for a long time. Time stopped. She suddenly leaped forth with one word: "Pastry."

"Okay . . ."

"I want to learn how to make fine pastry. Take the courses you take to become a real pastry chef. After I learned that I was going deaf I'd go out whenever I could and treat myself to fancy pastry at a good restaurant. I think most of us appreciate how delicious fancy desserts are, but I'd think, *Wow, someone actually made this.* We all have these, like, *If I could only do that* moments. I don't know why this never occurred to me before. Here's this thing I want to do, have a real skill that could never be taken from me, and I couldn't see it until now."

Lisa went on. "My issues with loss are not going to stop. Maybe this isn't even rational, but when something really bad happens, your sense of security is gone. That's the difference between people like me and everyone else. Something happened to me and it just, I don't know how to put it, it just *stopped* me. But I want to get unfrozen. And I think everything we learn unfreezes us. Anything that gives us a meaning—what it really does is unfreeze us from our pasts and give us a future."

All I could say was "Awesome!"

If you're like Lisa and you know that the meaning of what happened was to strengthen you, you, too, may be asking, "For what?"

The answer is that now is the time to dream. If something happened to you that was big enough to leave you hungry to understand its meaning and if you answered *yes* to four of the diagnostic questions here, it was big enough to strengthen you in an important way. And if you've been strengthened in an important way, then you now have the basis for something big in your life.

The bad event gave you the strength you needed in your foundation to make possible the next wonderful thing in your life.

So, for God's sake, don't blow it now. Dream your dream and make it happen. And if you don't know your dream yet, look at the way your foundation has been strengthened. That new foundation is probably pointing straight at what you want—something that you've not yet been able to admit to yourself.

Maybe I shouldn't talk about a dream. You know, for most of us it doesn't take much to give us a sense that we've redeemed our past. If it's something you care about or genuinely like, and it builds on the foundation strengthened by your loss, it will make you feel as if it's redeemed your past. But you have to go out there and make it real.

Making It Real

Insight without change is like an engagement without a marriage. It's all windup, no delivery. Insight is not a cure by itself. We have to turn a new vision into a new and better life.

I'm not saying it's easy to do. I'm not saying we even know *what* to do right away. But I deeply believe that finding a way to change ourselves or our lives is the point of our struggle to find meaning.

So don't cheapen the meaning of what you went through by failing to build on the new foundation you've been given.

I know this holds us to a tough standard. It's easier to think that some major insight by itself will rearrange the neurons in our brain and improve things. I wish it were that simple. But before we had that insight, we did things that hurt us and lived lives that weren't good for us. Our insight alone won't change what we do and how we live. Only change changes things.

Think of it like this: Suppose you're growing roses and they start dying because you don't know how to take care of them. Then suppose you make some discoveries about rose cultivation. That's great. But it won't do anything for the roses in your garden. You now have to use what you've learned to go out there and do some new and different things for your roses. Only then will they come back to life.

Are We Having Fun Yet?

————◆•◆•◆————

One of the most frequent comments people make after they've gone through tough times is "At least something good came out of it—I realized life is short, so I'd better enjoy it."

Sometimes the realization is a lot more specific. I've heard people say that their difficulties taught them that life is too precious not to be savored, so they need to spend more time traveling, fly fishing, dancing, hanging out with friends, lying on the beach, falling in love, reading great literature, or whatever is most enjoyable for them. This is the place where authenticity and pleasure meet.

You might say, *Yeah, but isn't "enjoy life" just a cliché?* Maybe, for people who already enjoy life. But as you'll see with Jim, it's not a cliché for people who don't find it easy to enjoy life. Maybe you're one of them.

Jim went through a lot to discover that for him being true to yourself and being able to enjoy life go hand in hand. Jim got into college on a football scholarship. His parents were certainly too poor to have been able to send him to college. Jim looked back on the life in which he'd been raised and it scared him. He vowed his life would be different. He would work hard, take care of business, and, like Scarlett O'Hara, never be "hungry" again.

Professional football was never in the cards for Jim. Instead he went to work for a large and influential local insurance agency. And *work* is the right word. Work would save him from the poverty he feared. He worked at finding the right woman to marry. He worked at having the right kind of relationship with her. He worked at bringing up his children in the right way. He worked at starting his own agency. And he worked at getting to know the kinds of people that would help his business.

Jim was one of those guys who, if you'd asked him if he was happy, would've said he never thinks about happiness, "but I guess I'm living right, so I must be happy." Then, as Jim put it, "Things started happening in my life." A teenage daughter got in trouble with drugs. His youngest child turned out to have a developmental disability. Jim was diagnosed with arthritis. Both of his parents died within a year of each other. His most important client dropped a lawsuit in his lap when the guy ended up being underinsured for some disaster he'd incurred.

Jim saw that he was in deep doo-doo when he found himself asking people, "Why is this happening to me?" It just didn't make any sense to him. Among other things, he'd thought of himself as a significant contributor to good causes, writing big checks every year to Catholic Charities and other philanthropies.

One day, in the hope that he might magically square things with God and stop his run of bad luck, Jim decided to volunteer in the pediatric cancer unit of a local hospital. He had vague Mother Teresa visions of himself mopping fevered brows. But the kids in the unit wanted to play. Even the sickest kids just wanted their lives to be a little more fun. But Jim couldn't help here. "You're no fun, Mister," was the verdict one girl delivered. And for the first time in his life Jim saw himself as failing at some activity he set out to do.

Here he was in this place of miracles and mystery, in an attempt to save his own life, and it was as if God himself were delivering a personal message to Jim through the lips of a sick little girl. It was as if Jim had gotten as far off the beaten track as it was possible to go and the only way back was through fun and play.

At first it felt like a curse. "But this is the one thing I'm worst at," Jim said in his prayers one Sunday morning. Later that day he found himself on the golf course, playing in a typical foursome of business friends. As usual, Jim's concentrated style of play was earning him a low score. Then he saw the other three guys laughing and kidding as they approached the tee for the eighteenth hole. *Oh, my God,* Jim thought, *I've been ruining my own life. I've just been playing golf this whole time. These guys have been having* fun. *Every time I win, I lose.*

The meaning of what had been happening to Jim suddenly

became clear. The last thing he needed to do was to square things with God by being an even more diligent duty doer. That was his strong suit already. What had been missing in Jim's life was what had been missing in Jim.

Here's what he told me: "I'd been a religious guy all my life, and I'd completely missed the point of it all. God had given me so many gifts, but they were all summed up in the gift of life itself. And the point of life was like the point of any gift—it's there for you to enjoy. By being so grim, Jeez, I've spent my life spurning God's gift. Everything in my life happened to bring me to those sick kids, and they taught me that I have a deep spiritual duty to enjoy myself as much as possible in this life God gave me."

So what did Jim do? Walk around with a lamp shade on his head and wear T-shirts with funny sayings? Of course not. For Jim, it was more like he *relaxed* away from the sense that he was responsible for everything. He relaxed *into* whatever opportunities there were for pleasure in his life. He was able to play because he found the play, the looseness, in everyday activities, the sense that he could let things go, let them take care of themselves, and let others take care of things, too. He started enjoying the people in his family that he'd spent so much time worrying about, and he realized that enjoyment was the only gift they'd ever really wanted from him.

Untying the Knots

Why does Cosmic Kindergarten go to enormous lengths to teach what should be a simple lesson? It's because enjoying life is what some people need to be fully and authentically themselves.

Really enjoying life doesn't have to mean running around doing new things. It often means allowing ourselves to get pleasure from our lives exactly as they are. But sometimes the only way to do that is to stop taking so seriously the very things that rob us of pleasure. I'm talking about the worries, ambitions, obsessions, confusions, distractions, and stresses that suck the blood of enjoyment out of what should be a happy life. I know—we too often feel we *have* to take these things seriously. It's what we think it means to be responsible. But we think this until some life-changing event comes along, puts it all in perspective, and shows us how wrong we were.

What about you? Here are the diagnostic questions:

- Deep down, do you feel you don't deserve to have fun?
- Growing up, did you get the message that life was grim and that work, not play, was the bedrock of existence?
- Have you always dreamed of really enjoying yourself one day but never gotten around to doing anything about it?
- Do people sometimes tell you that you take things too seriously?
- Is pleasure something you have to work at?
- Is it hard for you to enjoy yourself unless you can justify what you're doing with some practical payoff?

If you answered *yes* to four or more of these questions, then one of the reasons you went through what you did was to drive home the importance of enjoying yourself, enjoying life, and not taking things so seriously.

It's interesting, though: Sometimes the very people who need this lesson the most have the hardest time seeing and accepting it.

Eat Your Dessert

Big, life-changing events don't happen to us to bring us old news. The things that leave us hungry to discover the reason why—they are *life-changing* events. They teach us something we haven't known, or give us a gift we've never gotten before, or create an opportunity we've never even conceived of, if we can understand their meaning. That is how negative change gets transformed into positive change.

But, of course, it's the lessons we've been blind to that are hardest for us to learn. For many people, enjoying life is a complicated issue, one that touches on deep parts of the self. It brings up worries—if you're enjoying life, then you're not taking care of business. It brings up guilt—you don't deserve to enjoy life. It brings up insecurity—you don't have the inner resources necessary for enjoying life. Somehow while growing up you got the wrong messages or had the wrong experiences.

Let me tell you about Amy, who, as she put it, was "thirty-six with no kids and a bad attitude." She was a small, sweet-looking woman, more like the caricature of a librarian in her navy blue skirt and white man-tailored blouse than the police detective she actually was. It was only when she stood up and started walking around that you could see the steel of authority in her.

What happened to Amy? Some disasters unfold in super

slow motion, and that's how it was for her. Amy wanted to be married and have kids along with having work she cared about. But she had the misfortune of loving a series of men she'd thought loved her but who all turned out to be jerks. When she talked to them about getting married they all made it seem as if she was crazy and weak. They kept saying things like they weren't ready to commit. Then they dumped her.

"How did I get sucked into all this?" Amy asked. "My whole life is based on being able to trust myself. But I can't trust myself now knowing that I stayed in these stupid relationships for so long for no good reason at all."

Amy answered *yes* to all six of the diagnostic questions in this chapter. But she still didn't see how the meaning of what had happened to her could possibly be that she needed to enjoy life more. She didn't even want it to be the meaning. "To go through what I did just to see that I need to . . . *have fun?* That seems pretty silly as a reason for going through hell." Amy had been shown the truth, but she couldn't see it.

People don't forget to enjoy life the way you might forget your wallet when you leave the house. The idea that life is tough and you need to keep your shoulder to the wheel and your nose to the grindstone is a deeply ingrained attitude. People hold onto this attitude the way a man overboard holds onto a life preserver.

Think about the way many of us have grown up. Life was hard for many of our parents. They had troubles, and they suffered for whatever mistakes they made. If they managed to achieve some kind of success, they may have paid a big price for it. Worry and struggle were the keynotes of most of their days and most of their thoughts at night. Few of us had lighthearted parents.

Then we kids show up, and kids are all about goofing off and having fun. And that's when the antifun propaganda starts. "Quit fooling around." "What do you think this is, a joke?" "You better buckle down." Deep down, we sense an edge in our parents' voices. They really mean it. They're concerned. They're scared for us. Fun and pleasure are distractions at best, and too often pathways to failure.

This is why it's easy for so many of us to miss the fact that the reason something happened is to show us how important it is to enjoy life. *We're scared of thinking of life as something to be enjoyed.*

I knew it would be a challenge to bring Amy to the point where she could see this truth. "Let's go through some of the questions again," I said. "Is pleasure and enjoyment something you have to work at, for example?" (Everyone can use all the diagnostic questions in this book not just as diagnostic tools but as springboards for thinking about yourself and your life.)

"Oh, absolutely," Amy said. "I have a lot of trouble relaxing. I mean, I'll go out for a beer with some people after work and we'll talk, but I'm wanting to talk about work. I don't get small talk. Sometimes the other people start laughing and clowning around and it just makes me feel very alone. And at home I always want to be doing something. You know, sometimes I'll take a bath to relax, but I'll justify it as something that's good for me."

"Now what about this: Do you feel you don't deserve to have fun?"

Amy was silent for a moment. "I *think* I deserve to have fun, but I don't *feel* it."

"Why not?"

"I don't know how to put it. It's like, you can eat your dessert when you've finished your meal. I don't feel I've ever finished my meal. There's always something to do. I work in the serious-crimes unit. What I really feel is that I can start having fun when every murder's been solved and every missing child's been found."

"And, of course, they're never going to find every missing child."

"No, they're not," Amy said with sadness in her voice. "I was sort of a missing child. Or my childhood was missing from me. I never had a birthday party as a kid. One of my roommates wanted me to give her a birthday party and I just didn't know how. I mean, I knew that you get a cake and blow out the candles and get presents—you go to the store and buy them. But how do you actually make it happen? How do you know when to light the candles and give the gifts? How do you turn it into a celebration?"

"And you never learned stuff like this. No one ever did it for you."

"It wasn't that it just wasn't there. It was that it was some-how wrong and dangerous. It was like life was a loaded gun—you don't play with it."

"So it must be very hard for you to think that the meaning of what happened is that you have to start enjoying life. You don't know how to do that."

"Yeah, and I just don't get the connection between learning

to get pleasure from life and wasting a whole bunch of years hooking up with the wrong guys."

"Come on, Amy," I said. "Isn't the whole point of being in a relationship that you *enjoy it*? Don't you think you would've put an end to your relationships and all the pain and wasted time if you'd felt entitled to ask, *Wait a minute, am I having fun yet?* The whole point of what you went through was that if you remember how important it is to enjoy yourself, you're going to save yourself from putting up with an awful lot of painful crap."

Amy was silent again, her lower lip slightly tucked in like a child's. "I thought the point was I should've found a way to make my relationships work."

"Maybe the sign that they were bad relationships," I said more softly, "was that it always felt like so much work."

Everyone who answered *yes* to these diagnostic questions can see something similar for themselves.

Whatever it was you went through would've been a lot better, your life would've been a lot better, if extracting every ounce of joy from life had been a high priority for you.

Let Me Write You a Pleasure Prescription

Amy went on to say something that I thought was really striking. "Can I confess something?" she said. "I think part of me doesn't want this to be the meaning of what happened to me because I really don't know what to do about it. This is a part of life where I feel clueless."

It's not always easy to apply the lessons you learn in Cosmic

Kindergarten. A lot of people are in Amy's situation. They get it—they need to kick back and start enjoying life—but they think they don't know how to do that. And then they shrug their shoulders and give up.

Big mistake. Enjoying life isn't just the cherry on top of the icing on top of the cake: *It's the whole cake.* Enjoyment doesn't have to be silly. You might genuinely enjoy yourself most when you're helping someone in trouble, or discovering something in a laboratory, or reading a child a bedtime story. But the part of your psyche that motivates you thrives on your enjoying yourself. Enjoyment is the food of motivation. When you don't enjoy yourself, your sense of being motivated gradually withers.

If you want to have more genuine pleasure, *the first step is to let go of the past.* It makes sense that many of us get stuck not being able to let go of the past. But, you might say, the thing that happened was something bad. What do you do—just shrug your shoulders and walk away from it?

I know it's difficult, but people who successfully let go of the past stop making a shrine out of whatever happened. And there are a million ways we have of turning our pasts into shrines. Even therapy can be a shrine like this. It's true that if someone's had a very unhappy childhood it may be useful to talk to someone and get help. But when this goes on for years and years, it becomes clear that moving on is not the goal. This kind of therapy has now become the shrine in which the sad past is worshiped.

Let's take a mother who keeps her child's room exactly the way it was the day he died. She's made a shrine of it. She can truly come to believe that there is some meaning in what happened—although never a justification, of course—and she can know in her heart what that meaning is. But at some point she's got to get up, go in that room, and dismantle that shrine. That means throwing some stuff away, putting some other stuff in boxes, and maybe putting other things in a scrapbook. And then she has to turn that space into a room that can be used by the living.

That's *doing* something, and it's always the hardest for people. When it comes to discovering the meaning of what happened to us, the meaning alone is great and makes a real difference, but it won't change our lives until we dismantle our own shrines, whatever they are.

What are our shrines? Whatever we use to make the present serve the past. There is a difference between a shrine and a commemoration. If someone you love dies, of course you're going to want to keep photographs of that person. You're just commemorating the past. But if you spend all day kneeling in front of those photographs, your present is being destroyed to serve the past.

I understand how hard it is to dismantle a shrine. But if you want to discover the change that needs to happen, you have to identify your shrine. What is it in your life that represents your holding onto your loss, identifying with it, making it part of who you are? That's your shrine.

How do you dismantle it? You do something different. Do anything but what you've been doing. You find a way to live differently. If you've been living in the shrine of your loss, *making* this change is hard, but you already know *what* you need to do.

After you've let go of the past, you need to move forward strongly into the future.

The second step is to identify genuine sources of play and pleasure in your life. You'd have to be a pretty grim person not to have these sources. We were all kids once, and even those of us with really tough childhoods can figure out some ways to have fun sometimes!

These experiences of pleasure and fun are a real foundation. They are sense memories, not buried at all, but just sort of lost amid the piles of paper on our mental desks. But they are within arm's reach.

You can use your ability to work hard and take things seriously by using your strengths to fix your weaknesses. Your answers to the diagnostic questions tell you that enjoying yourself is medicine for your heart that you need to take to save your life. So write yourself a pleasure prescription. Roll up your sleeves and go to work putting more enjoyment in your life.

A good way to begin is to keep a pleasure diary. It doesn't have to be a big deal or take much time. The key is tracking the truth about pleasure in your everyday life. Just as there can be a huge difference between the way we think we eat (pretty healthfully) and the way we actually eat (*Wow, I didn't realize I ate so many empty calories*), there are usually big and important surprises in store when we see—morning to night, at work and at home, alone and with other people, week in and week out—how much pleasure there really is in our lives and where we actually get it.

As you keep your pleasure diary, note some of the following:

- For the next seven days, what's the one moment in each day where you got the most true, clear pleasure?
- Who in your life gives you the most pleasure? What kind of pleasure is that?
- How much time did you spend this week giving yourself pleasure of any kind? What was most disappointing? Where did you get the biggest bang for the buck?
- What kind of pleasure daydreams come up most often for you?

Hunt for the tiny, fleeting, pleasure-pointing if-only's that pop into your head. These are the thoughts that say, *If I could only do that, then I'd really be enjoying myself.* They will tell you which pleasures are missing in your life.

The point is to note anything that hints at the possibility of finding more things to enjoy, and new ways of enjoying what already exists in your life.

No one can teach us how to enjoy life. *We can only teach ourselves* and it's important to know that you *can* teach yourself. You already know a lot about enjoying life, more than you think, and you can build on what you know.

How to Change

There are plenty of Amys in the world. This mind-set is very common among immigrant kids like me, for example, or children whose parents had more than their share of worries. It's not that we can't laugh and be happy, it's just that fun doesn't come easily to us. So "What exactly do I do?" is a question we need to respect.

What people like this have to see is that there's nothing wrong with them. There's no constitutional defect. On some level it's no different from never having learned to ride a bicycle. You can learn at any time. It always feels weird and impossible at first, but you keep trying, you fall off a lot, you get hurt a few times, and then you get it. You do it wrong until you do it right, trusting that as you do it wrong some instinct inside will bring you to the point where you'll do it right. But you have to keep doing it over and over.

This is how change happens for people, and too much of the time we suffer for not understanding this. We mistakenly think of change as feeling differently on the inside. That's what we look for. That's what we try to make happen. But changing from the inside out is as easy as ... why don't you try this? Stand up. Bend over. Grab both ankles. Now lift yourself up.

So, how'd you do? I'm betting you were barely able to lift yourself more than an inch or so off the floor. Seriously, it's impossible, of course.

And it's equally impossible to change yourself from the inside out.

Real change happens from the outside in. I know that from my own clinical experience and research and from the work of countless other professionals. And this is good news because we *know* how to make changes on the outside. *No one* knows how to reach in and directly make changes on the inside. So, here's how you make real change.

First, think about where you want to end up. Let's say you were to change a lot. Where would that take you? How would you know that you'd changed? What would you see? What would other people see? You're looking for behaviors here, specific things you do.

Second, do things that have a chance of bringing about this change. Take small but meaningful steps in the right direction. Everything that brings you closer to where you want to end up is good. It's more important to do *something* than to do something perfect. Keep trying different things until you get it.

For example, let's say you've gotten feedback that you're just not a fun person. And you're afraid that it's true. You look inside yourself and see someone who's all about responsibilities, not fun. But how do you become a fun person? Well, you know that if you were a fun person people would see you doing fun things. So that's what you do. Even though you haven't experienced any inner change, you just try to do all the fun things you can, to the best of your ability.

Third, ignore the fact that in spite of what you're doing you don't feel you've changed all that much on the inside yet.

Fourth, keep on doing things that have a chance of bringing about the change you want.

Finally, one day you'll wake up and you'll realize that you've changed. Finally your insides will be different because your actions have been different for quite a while.

Don't fight it. If you want to change, this is the way to go, from the outside in. And this is how you change yourself into someone who gets every ounce of pleasure from life.

Anyone who found out that learning to enjoy life more was a reason they went through what they did should accept that reconnecting with the pleasure instinct will take time. But, hey, poor you—having to try many different things to have as much fun as possible! Some of the pleasurable things you do will really be quite enjoyable. Keep doing them.

Here's a little tip. Maybe you know someone who really knows how to enjoy life, or you can imagine someone like that. Let's call that person Pat. Let Pat be your internal fun guide. You find you have a whole Sunday with nothing to do. You were going to spend the day doing chores. Instead imagine what Pat would do. Pat will know what's fun. Do that.

The Gift of Pleasure

The last step is to silence the voices in your head that make pleasure painful.

There's the voice of fear. It says that whenever you're enjoying life, you're not taking care of what has to be done. Your business will go to hell. Your clients will get into trouble. Your family will fall apart.

Here's what you say to this voice. "Enjoying life is one thing. Letting my life go to hell is something completely different. I'll never let my life go to hell. But in a sense I have let my life go to hell by depriving myself of pleasure. I'm not going to let 'taking care of business' serve as an excuse for not getting pleasure from my life."

You might have to deal with the impact of fear on your ability to have fun one situation at a time. The minute you see that your fear is starting to interfere with your fun ask yourself, *What's the harm here?* Before, you only enjoyed yourself if you had an ironclad guarantee that nothing would be neglected in any way. What you're going to do now is always enjoy yourself unless there's a very powerful and particular reason not to.

197

Then there's the voice of guilt. It says you don't deserve to enjoy life. Many people suffer from an Atlas complex. They're carrying the world on their shoulders and they'd feel terribly guilty if they put it down to have fun.

So, here's what to do. Think of your life as a precious gift from God, from the universe. And God gave you the gift of life for you to enjoy it. He may have had other reasons, too, but having pleasure is one of the core reasons. Instead of feeling guilty when you enjoy yourself, feel guilty about dishonoring the gift of life when you're not enjoying yourself. Even better, don't feel guilty. Just enjoy.

Some people feel guilty because they can't forget that someone somewhere is suffering. If that's spoiling your ability to enjoy life, here's what I suggest. Either help those people you feel guilty about so they can start enjoying life or start enjoying life yourself. But sitting there feeling guilty doesn't help anyone. And I'll go even further. Be careful about helping people if you get no pleasure from it. When caregivers have trouble enjoying life, they bring a grim, even mean-spirited quality to their caregiving. Think about this. Suppose you were dying in a hospice, God forbid. Who would you want helping you? Someone who was filled only with a sense of duty? Or someone who was deeply connected to the pleasures life has to offer?

Finally, some people are held back because there's a voice that tells them they don't have the inner resources necessary for enjoying life. Usually people feel this way because they know that somehow growing up they got the wrong messages or had the wrong experiences.

Well, you know, even Dickens didn't mostly have a

Dickensian childhood. Kids who grow up in really tough circumstances find amazing opportunities to have fun. If you were a kid, then you have all the inner resources you need. So tell that voice to shut up. What you need are more experiences of pleasure now. Go out and get them.

Placing the Rose

REASON 9: TO SHOW YOU HOW TO LIVE
WITH A SENSE OF MISSION

———————•◆•———————

When she was thirteen, Katharine Hepburn found the body of her beloved older brother. He'd just committed suicide by hanging himself.

Therapist types used to wring their hands about a tragedy like this. They'd focus on how Katharine Hepburn would be psychologically scarred by this event. But people are tougher than they've been given credit for. This event was surely big enough to have a huge impact on Hepburn, but its meaning didn't come from the damage it did but from the lessons Hepburn learned: Life is incredibly precious, you never know how much life is left you, and you can't waste your life any more than you'd waste the water in the last canteen if you were traveling in the desert.

So Hepburn lived the rest of her life as if she were a woman with a mission. You know what people with a mission are like. They live life with a special intensity. It's as if they feel they have more to do than the rest of us, or as if what they have to do is more important than what the rest of us do. If life is a poker game, we're the ones playing penny ante while they're playing for huge stakes.

People can focus this kind of special intensity on anything. Having a mission isn't only for life's activists, people who passionately believe in some cause and are willing to spend much of their life fighting for it. Hepburn's mission was her acting career. Scarlett O'Hara had a mission: "As God is my witness, I'll never go hungry again." Okay, okay, Scarlett O'Hara was a fictional character, but plenty of us have developed the very same mission if we were victims of devastation. My mother had the same mission as Scarlett O'Hara; she lived her life with the same intensity, and the reason was that she, too, had witnessed her life and her world go up in flames.

Other people might find meaning in what happened to them by burning with an intense desire to see that all of their children go to college and make something of their lives. There are artists who work with a special intensity, as if every painting they complete were like a masterpiece they risked their life to save from a burning building. There are even people whose mission is simply to experience life to the fullest, whose hunger to see the world is filled with a special intensity.

Most of us admire people like that. But when we think about having a mission that drives us forward and takes over our lives, most of us feel ambivalent.

A Cup of Fire

Intensity's great, but who wants to live life on fire? Who wants the struggle and sacrifice that come with having a mission? Who wants the inevitable frustration and defeats that come with dealing with powerful forces? Even Jesus didn't always feel up for his mission. He spent his twenties avoiding the high-intensity living he must have known was his destiny. Later, fully appreciating what he'd gotten himself into, he said, "May this cup pass from me," responding as anyone would to the mission entrusted to him.

For most of us, there's enough struggle just living a regular life. Who needs to go forth and battle dragons?

But we're also powerfully drawn to the idea of living a life emblazoned with passion. I think that's mostly because we're aware of the abyss of meaninglessness that can so easily lie at our feet. You know—like when out of the corner of your mind's eye you catch a glimpse of the idea that you're born, you work, you have a few laughs, and then you die, and what was it all for? Sometimes I think it's the best people among us who are most prone to a hunger for meaning. They sense that life can be most full of life when it's based on a struggle to make life better.

So part of us hungers for a sense of mission, part of us fears the cost. Usually it's the fear part of us that wins. Everyday life is in the driver's seat. We live, we laugh, we take things as they come. And that's okay.

But some of us need a sense of mission. We may not want it, but to become who we were meant to be we need to be driven by some passionate conviction, some vision of living life to the fullest. We, too, pray that the cup may pass from us. But then some personal disaster or painful problem comes along and accomplishes what all the good intentions in the world were not able to accomplish. It gives us permission to unshackle the intensity we're capable of bringing to life. And this, for the first time, makes life feel meaningful in a whole new way.

Let's not look for any simplistic connection between the event and the sense of mission that comes from it. Katharine Hepburn didn't spend her life as an activist against teen suicide. Just because your grandma got run over by a bus doesn't mean you're going to start a crusade against out-of-control bus drivers.

The need to live life with a special intensity (and this might involve fighting for a cause) comes from who we are as people, not from the specific event we went through.

Take the Protestant and Catholic mothers whose children were killed by sectarian violence on the streets of Belfast and Londonderry, Northern Ireland. All these mothers hated what had killed their children. All of them needed to find meaning in what had happened. All of them needed to find a way to deal with their loss. But only some of them discovered that their anger transformed itself into a cause they could fight for— campaigning, marching, protesting to prevent more bloodshed.

It's not that some mothers cared and others didn't. They all cared. But the small percentage of the mothers who seized on the cause of ending bloodshed in Northern Ireland had some hunger that this cause satisfied. Fighting for a cause was part of the life they'd always been meant to live.

Some of these mothers developed a sense of mission we never saw. It wasn't a mission to fight for a cause, though—it was a mission to take their families the hell out of there so they could lead a better life. Some saw the waste of life and simply decided that in whatever way meant most to them they would live their lives with an intensity they'd never known before.

We all know people who are driven by passion. When I was a college freshman, I became friends with the woman who lived across the hall from me. Ronnie studied more passionately than anyone I knew, not like a nerd but like someone with a mission. One day I was in her room. While we were talking, she murmured, "Excuse me," and then as if it were the most natural thing in the world she pulled out a syringe and gave herself an injection.

I'd never seen anything like that before. I was too shy then to ask her what this was all about. But she was used to talking to people about it. She was very open. It turned out that she'd been giving herself insulin shots since she was eight. Being diagnosed with diabetes as a child had made her aware of how much doctors can help people and how much people needed their help. And so her personal medical problem gave Ronnie a huge sense of mission.

Every little girl who develops a serious medical condition does not become fueled with a passion to rid the world of disease. Ronnie did. It was what she needed.

The only problem with Ronnie's story is that it might seem a little too pat: sick girl becomes doctor to help other sick girls. Most of the time life is less predictable than that, full of sur-

EVERYTHING HAPPENS FOR A REASON

prising twists. There often doesn't seem to be a connection between what happens to a person and the passion for life that arises as a result.

Grace's Mission

Since she was a child, Grace was quite overweight. When she graduated from college she weighed two hundred pounds. The one thing that angered her more than anything else was people who talked to her as if losing weight was a new idea, as if she hadn't had many painful, disastrous experiences with diets, fat camps, you name it.

As a young woman she decided that all she could do was accept herself exactly as she was. Grace knew it would be tough to find a guy who could see beyond her "alternative image" of feminine beauty. But she hoped for the best.

Years passed. Dates were few and far between. Grace had a couple of brief relationships. But it was tough, particularly since as a music-industry publicist she ran with an image-conscious crowd. She found that the guys she went out with who didn't mind her being so overweight were either weird or had self-image problems. "You see," Grace said to me, "I literally wouldn't want to belong to a club that would have me for a member." She seemed to have a sense of humor about her situation, but there was a deep sadness below the surface.

The part that really got to her was her sense of the waste of it all. She knew she was a really good person with a lot of love to give. And yet she might never move off the shelf because of a problem with the packaging. Grace found she was deeply moved whenever she heard stories of people with untapped potential sitting on a shelf somewhere going to waste.

Then she saw that there was more than one way to feel like a waste and more than one way to do something about it. Her being someone with a lot of energy, talent, and desire to help was also a waste, and yet she was doing nothing about it. Through her work she'd caught a glimpse of talented young women from disadvantaged backgrounds who had no way of creating a future in the music industry for themselves. They needed help, advice, mentoring. Some of them needed to be shown ways to turn talent into a marketable product. Others needed to be shown alternative ways of having careers in the music industry. Otherwise what they had to offer would go to waste.

So Grace had a moment of grace. She had a vision of living life more intensely. She put her free time into starting a non-profit organization that would reach out into the neighborhoods and give these young women the help Grace knew they needed. Grace worked with both music-industry movers and shakers as well as community leaders to get the funding. She also directly mentored and counseled girls herself. "I love it," Grace said to me. "It always makes me feel so much better than you'd think something like this would. It makes me feel good because I really think we're saving so many of these girls from wasting their lives and their talents."

As smart and self-aware as Grace was, she initially couldn't see that the wonderful work she did and the way it made her feel was the meaning of what she'd gone through as an overweight woman in America today.

I felt I needed to push Grace to help her see. "Okay, then," I said, "now complete the sentence 'Everything happens for a reason, and the reason I've lived through this really difficult situation of feeling unattractive and not being in a relationship was . . .'"

"I guess so I could help disadvantaged kids find their way in the music business."

"Okay, but now let's get at the deeper meaning. I think the reason you've had such a personal struggle was so you could find something you passionately believed in, and I think the reason this needed to happen the way it did is because I think this is something that scares you."

"Whoa," Grace said. "What do you mean?"

"There you were, just starting out as an adult. You're working and you see all these kids you know who don't have a chance. It had to be heartbreaking. And tell me if I'm wrong, but you had to have been thinking, *I've got to do something about this*, but you also must have seen that there was little that you as one person could do. Now I'm really going out on a limb here, but I'm thinking that somehow when you were growing up you got the message that you weren't important if you didn't do something big."

Grace jumped on this. "You know what my parents used to say to me when I'd come crying to them because someone made fun of me for being fat? They'd say, 'You'll show them.' And the more often I cried or the worse the incident, the more they made a big deal about how I was going to show them all one day. You know, I don't think the whole time I was growing up that I knew what it meant to 'show them.' But yeah, I always felt I was going to have to do something big. But it all got so tied up in my image of myself. That's why I think I had to become successful in this really cool business. I needed a big hit of both success and coolness to really show them. But that was for them.

"Working with these disadvantaged girls really was for *me*. I wasn't pleasing anyone except myself. I mean, suppose I'd never been fat. I often wonder about that. You know, you never know, but I keep thinking that my parents pressuring me all the time to 'show them' wasn't just about my being fat. I think I would've been under that kind of pressure under any conditions. It's just how my parents were. And I'm not so sure I wasn't Little Miss Superficial myself growing up.

"Maybe I needed to experience what it was like to be downtrodden to be able to care about people who were downtrodden so I could do something that could show *me* I really did have something special to offer. Not just cool, but truly valuable. It's so funny. I'd always thought of my body as a trap. Now I see how in another way it let me out of a trap."

Waking Up to Your Mission

Maybe you're like Grace. The meaning of what you went through was so you could discover your mission, and you've already discovered it. Or maybe this is your meaning but you haven't yet discovered your mission—maybe the very idea that you have a mission is a new one for you.

Either way, you need to see if this is the reason why you've gone through what you did. Please answer the following diagnostic questions to see if this reason fits you:

- Have you always had in the back of your mind a desire to make a sacrifice for something you believe in?
- Growing up, did you get the message that you have to do something big and important with your life?
- Do you sometimes feel you have to justify your existence, as if just living your life and not hurting anyone weren't enough?
- Is feeling proud of yourself something that matters a great deal to you? And when you think of feeling proud of yourself does it always feel connected to doing something that will make a difference?
- Have your heroes typically been people whose lives are defined by the intensity with which they lived or how they stood up for what they believed in?

If you answer *yes* to three or more of these questions, then the reason you've gone through what you've gone through is so you'd be freed up to live your life with a special intensity, based on something you wanted to accomplish or a way you wanted to live.

This doesn't mean you have to devote your entire life to fighting for a cause. And it doesn't mean that the cause has to be one that's meaningful to anyone but you. It could be volunteering at your church, synagogue, mosque, or temple. It could be working with your neighbors to plant flowers to make your street beautiful. It could be traveling to every remote corner of the world. It could be living in such a way that you never have time for television.

The point is, though, that you're not doing it just to keep busy or because your friends are doing it. You're doing it because you see deep within it something that gives meaning to your life. And you know you need more of a sense of meaning.

Beyond Guilt

Finding your passion has nothing to do with guilt either. It's true that some people who've gone through tough events feel guilty. As I know all too well myself, they may feel guilty that they've survived, or that they didn't prevent what happened. There are many reasons. Sometimes when we feel guilty we feel we need to do something to expiate our guilt.

But here's what I've learned: If finding a cause to believe in and fight for is *not* the reason something happened to you, then it won't do anything for your feelings of guilt to fight for it. So you don't need to feel guilty for not taking up a cause, because this is not what you were meant to do.

But if this is a reason for you, then finding something you believe in that you want to do something about will give you more than just relief from guilt. It will give you hope and direction because you'll have found your meaning.

Finding Your Passion

For many people this revelation—that the meaning of what happened is so they can live life with a special intensity—is all they need. Now they can understand why they've been living with so much intensity. Other people now find that they can make sense of feelings that were a mystery—*oh, so that's what I've been missing: I've been needing to live life with full intensity; no wonder I felt so restless and stifled.* Still other people might now feel they have permission to actually go forth and act on the sense of mission they've always known they've had.

Some people, though, need a little something more at this

point. They understand the meaning of what happened to them. They can feel their need to live with a sense of intensity. But they don't know where to take their passion. They don't know what their passion is.

It's hard to miss a mission—if you've got one, you know what it is. But if you don't know what your mission is yet, how do you discover it?

This is an important question. All my years working with people have shown me that lots of us have a desire to do something special with our lives . . . and that's where we stop. Special how? Where? With whom? We don't have a clue. We know what we care about, but we usually care about too many things and we don't know what to do with our caring. After all, mission means having one specific thing you care about and a focused way to act on your caring.

I know personally how tough it can be to identify your mission. As a child of Holocaust survivors, I was haunted by many of the same concerns other people like me had. We didn't want anything like the Holocaust to ever happen again. We didn't want people to forget what had happened. We wanted the needs of the survivors to be taken care of. And as we realized that the children of survivors had needs, too, we wanted to address those needs as well.

So when I was thirty, I joined an organization called One Generation After. It was a way for children of Holocaust survivors to come together and do something about the concerns I've just mentioned. Finally I had a cause! And I threw myself into it, as I do with everything. I became head of the group's speakers bureau and gave talks everywhere.

I was so happy to be involved in something I believed in so

much. But then a process of discovery started that I couldn't have predicted.

When you have a cause, you have to attend meetings. What I found was that I truly hated meetings. And then I hated myself for hating the meetings. What kind of child of Holocaust survivors was I if couldn't stand meetings when our parents had withstood so much?

There was clearly a conflict between my sense of my mission and what was required to carry it out. This all came to a head when I was asked to represent our group at a very special event in Israel. Holocaust survivors and their children, relatives, and friends all came together for a historic commemoration. The emotional highlight was to be an event at which everyone placed a red rose on a special site at the Holocaust museum in Jerusalem. So we could all do this, thousands of us had to stand on a long line for hours in the hot sun.

As I stood in line, my rose and I wilting under the sun, something in me rebelled against this mission I thought I had. It was a mission that originated in people's being made victims. It was about their victimhood. It was about my placing this victimhood close to the heart of who I was.

And I saw that this mission was not *me*, in the deepest possible sense. My entire career as a therapist, researcher, and writer has been about fighting people's sense that they're defined by their victimhood. The very reason I'm writing this book is to help people come to terms with some event from their past so they can let it go and move forward, once they've extracted from it the lesson it had to teach them.

Finally my turn came. I placed my rose on top of all the others. Soon it would be lost under all the roses carried by the people behind me. And I knew I was done with this mission that had never really been mine.

Staring out the window on the flight home, I realized something new about the meaning of my surviving when so many others had died. I came back from my trip with a total shift in focus. I did have a cause to fight for. I needed a cause to fight for. But commemorating the past wasn't my cause. In my entire life I'd never had a hero whose life was devoted to remembering the past. All my heroes had been people who'd saved lives. But I was already saving lives, in my own way, as a therapist. I could never save the lives of the people who died in the Holocaust. I could never give my mother a childhood in which she was loved and taken care of or a youth that was filled with hopes for anything other than survival. But I could help other people.

So we don't always know our passion when we're starting out. It's easy to think something is our passion when it really isn't. But what can you do? If you know your passion, you know it. But if all you know is that the reason something happened is so you can have a sense of mission, all you can do is make your best guess, throw yourself into it, see how it feels, and if it doesn't feel right, find something else. This is exactly what everyone else who's found his or her passion has done. But don't sit around waiting for it to come to you.

I do have three strong pieces of advice for people who are looking for a way to focus their enormous intensity. I base this advice on stories I've accumulated over the years of people who are happy with their missions in life.

First, *think small and close to home.* The personal and the immediate always seem to be more meaningful to people than something abstract and remote. This is why, for example, people often take up a mission connected to people and events that touch their lives personally. Also, by thinking small and close to home you're more likely to act. Now you can understand why so many people who are fueled by their own intensity start their own small businesses.

Second, *it's actions, not good intentions, that produce satisfaction.* After her husband died of colon cancer, Katie Couric had a colonoscopy live on the *Today* show to dramatize how important it was for people to get themselves checked and how doing so was not as big an ordeal as some think. If you don't know what to do with your sense of mission, don't worry, most people aren't sure what to do. But if you do *something*, no matter what, you'll be more fulfilled, plus you'll learn more about in what direction to go. It doesn't have to be a gigantic commitment. I'm just talking about doing *something.*

And third, *please yourself.* This might seem like strange advice. But finding a full-intensity life isn't always about helping others. Your mission can also include helping yourself. The people who've accomplished the most and gotten the greatest satisfaction out of their sense of mission were the ones who most listened to and tried to please themselves.

I think, for example, of an Englishwoman, Gladys Aylward, the heroine of the book and movie *The Inn of the Sixth Happiness,* which is based on her life. She was an uneducated servant, but she had a dream of serving as a missionary in China. Only that would please her. Every possible roadblock was thrown in her way. But she wouldn't let anyone talk her out of her dream. Eventually she got to China, where she did amazing work caring for children and saving their lives.

If there's a contradiction between what you have to do to please yourself and what it means to think small and close to home, please yourself first.

Huge Jars of Candy

———◆•◆•◆———

Nothing gives you a good life like being a good person.

Lots of people will never be able to understand this. It's not that they're bad people. But they're tone deaf to genuine goodness. They hurt others without ever realizing it. A million opportunities for doing something genuinely good pass them by and they never see a single one of them. Sure, they have possessions, they take trips, there are people in their lives. But there's a kind of hollow grayness that they'll never escape because they lack the ability to become truly good people.

Some of us, though, are also living in this hollow grayness, deprived of the bright, sweet life that belongs to people who are truly good. But we're *not* trapped forever. We have untapped resources for goodness we've never known about until something happens in life to wake us up.

I'll never forget Roger. He was about as rich and handsome as can be. He seemed like a pretty good guy, too, in a careless, somewhat lazily self-centered way: He'd never deliberately hurt someone, he'd write checks for causes if you asked him, but he rarely went out of his way to help anyone.

Roger was totally devastated because his young wife had decided to get out of their marriage.

As I got to know him my picture of him changed. Roger was not as good a guy as he thought he was. For all the gifts nature had bestowed on him, Roger didn't do much to pay back for what he had. And in a clumsy, inadvertent way, he'd actually hurt a number of people—he'd dropped old friends, made cutting comments to associates. His wife had left him because of a number of casual cruelties—nothing shocking, just thoughtless instances of neglect and the occasional outburst of anger.

While he'd mistreated others, he'd been mistreated even worse himself. His father had bullied him. Nothing like child abuse, but his father had been perfectly willing to hurt him to make a man of him, ignoring the hurt that's inflicted when a boy gets the sense that he needs to be hurt if he's going to be made a man.

Roger came to me looking for some explanation for what had happened to him. Preferably it would have been a story about why his wife was crazy. He would have accepted a story about his having psychological issues of his own. Imagine his surprise when he saw that the reason why he'd lost the woman he loved was to teach him a lesson about becoming a truly good man.

Roger had been an excellent basketball player, and he was used to accepting what the coach told him to do. So he accepted what I told him like a good team player, and he worked his butt off to be as good a person as his imagination could conceive. He kept his eyes open for people in his life who might have problems he could help them with and he became a Big Brother. Within a year he was happier than he'd ever been in his life.

It doesn't always take a big personal catastrophe to teach a big lesson. My friend Viv was walking home one evening when she turned a corner and saw people clustered around a guy who'd evidently dropped dead of a heart attack. Of course Viv was upset seeing this. But still, she didn't know him from Adam, so why was this so *meaningful* to her?

Here's what she told me: "When I saw that guy lying there turning gray, *bang!*, I immediately thought that it could so easily have been me. I've got to start becoming a better person if you can die like that at any moment."

I can identify with this myself. There are moments when I believe that I'm a good person. I never deliberately hurt anyone. I try to help people whenever I can. But let's be honest: I'm a good person, but I'm also lazy. It could easily be true that there's a lot more I could do to be a lot better person. I also think good people care about doing good, and so we notice all the little ways in which we don't live up to our own standards. Or do I notice all these little moral lapses because I really am not as good a person as I think I am?

It's hard to know, isn't it? Even if the easy answer is *Yes, you're a good person*, when you look more closely, who knows?

Good, Better, Best

I know what you're thinking: *How does this apply to me? I'm a pretty darn good person already! Why would something happen to me to teach me that I need to become a better person?*

I know. I believe you. But it's not about whether you've earned enough points to rest on your laurels because you've earned "good person" status. It's about living up to your potential for being an even better person, your best possible self in fact, someone who isn't good in a soft, halfhearted way but in a strong, committed way.

Barbara Bush had been a very good person in the years before her husband became president. But then she went through an experience she describes as six months of the deepest depression, where she felt she'd wasted her life and lost her desire to live. Instead of getting help she merely stayed in that depressed state, which eventually lifted, thank God.

She describes how this experience made her a better person. Before, when she'd seen people going through tough times, she'd been judgmental because they hadn't just "snapped out of it." But now she'd learned her lesson. No one stays suffering like that because of a willful refusal to snap out of it. Barbara Bush had a revelation about how hard it can be for people to lift themselves out of their difficulties. The reason she'd gone through her own painful experience was to get a compassion transplant, something many of us need from time to time.

My research showed that there was one thing common to everyone who realized that the meaning of what happened was that they needed to work harder at being a truly good person.

It was seeing that others suffered as a result of the bad things they'd done. And what's more, that they'd typically been mistreated themselves. So they also knew what it was like to be on the receiving end.

That's the diagnostic here. One simple question:

+ Have you experienced loss or pain in your life both because you've been mistreated *and* because you've mistreated others?

If you answer *yes* to this diagnostic question, then the meaning of what happened to you is to help you see how important it is for you to become a better person—not just a little better, but an actively good person.

Being Good and Doing Well

It's hard for some people to accept that this applies to them. For example, when you're growing up in a poor neighborhood the way I did, you're always wondering if you're going to make it, which deep down means doing something that makes you proud of yourself. You know that your little world has a way of trapping you, limiting your hopes and opportunities, sucking you back into its mud. You see young people older than yourself, good-looking, bright, charming, and then one day there they are, married and living in the neighborhood, with kids of their own, working at a go-nowhere job. You know how hard it is to do really well. So being a good person can fall low on your ladder of priorities.

Sharon was a friend of mine growing up, one of those kids

you knew was going to do something big one day. She had that focus that makes all the difference, plus she had real talent.

Sharon's parents were garment-factory workers. Sharon wanted to be a designer. In her loose-leaf notebook she was always sketching skinny, long-necked, blank-faced women wearing all kinds of beautiful clothes, from ball gowns to tailored suits. When you see an eleven-year-old girl drawing women wearing tailored suits, you know she's serious.

And Sharon did make it. She got hot in the early eighties, becoming a much-talked-about young designer. With parents in the garment industry she knew the business, so she made a lot of money, too. In fact, she had it all, including a well-connected Wall Street husband.

The thing is, if you'd known her back when all this was starting, you'd have liked her a lot. Contrary to the image of people who claw their way out of the jungle, Sharon's success was accompanied by the fact that she was a genuinely good person. If a friend asked her for help, Sharon was there for her. And Sharon had never deliberately hurt anyone on her way up.

But as she got busy, she got less interested in being a good person. She'd rarely go out of her way to help anyone. Being good meant nothing more than not being bad and every once in a while writing a check she could easily afford. And still she thought of herself as a good person.

Then something happened to Sharon that devastated her. She got a call from her lawyer. Her husband had told his lawyer to tell her lawyer to tell her that he'd decided to get out of their marriage. And he wanted custody of their two boys.

He didn't think her "lifestyle" was good for the boys because all she did was work, he claimed, and hang out with weirdos.

The next three years were worse than if her husband had died. On top of her loss was a sense of rejection, a terrible fear of losing her children, and an inability to figure out why this was happening to her that ate away at Sharon like worms on a corpse. All she could get from her husband was that he didn't want to be married to her anymore, along with some vague references to terrible things she'd done.

It was about five years after this period that she called me. I'd been out of touch with Sharon, but I'd heard about some of her troubles through the grapevine. I was surprised that the woman I was looking at as we sat down for dinner radiated emotional energy.

After Sharon filled me in on everything that had happened, she continued, "But I'm okay now; more than okay. There was a period when I didn't know if I'd get out with my sanity. And even after things got clear and I ended up with joint custody, I was still devastated. It was such a deep rejection and I was so scared. Of course I felt terrible about myself. I thought, *What the hell's wrong with me? Am I this bad person?* But I'd always, always thought of myself as a really good person.

"Then this thing happened at work. There was this guy who'd been responsible for our production in the Far East, but he just didn't know the Far East. He couldn't deal with the people there. They were eating us up alive. He was an older guy. I had one of my vice presidents fire him. She came back and told me how he took it really hard and how hard it had been for her. I was still fed up and I said, 'Well, if you can't stand the heat get out of the kitchen. I can't play nursemaid for people.'

"My vice president—she'd started the business with me—just looked at me like, *Who the hell are you? I don't even know you.* And she walked out. It was her attitude of not thinking she could even begin to deal with me, like I was a lost cause—*that's* what really said something to me.

"I didn't know who to talk to. I went to see my aunt who'd been like a second mother to me. And I asked her, 'Aunt Rose, am I a good person?'

"She sighed. *Oh that's great!* I thought. *What a recommendation!* So I asked her to let me have it. And she said, 'Look, Sharon, you've been a very lucky person. You have a lot of gifts. You used to try hard to be good. But now I think you've hurt a lot of people without paying much attention to what you're doing.'"

Sharon suddenly saw a lot of things she'd never seen before. She was starting to turn into one of those cold, hard women who complain that no one sees how vulnerable they feel inside. She saw that maybe the best part of her had gotten lost. She said to herself, *I don't want to be someone who at best was merely not evil. I want to be a positively good person—you know, really do good things.*

The woman I saw sitting across from me was a woman who had transformed herself. Sharon realized that her husband had been the canary in the coal mine. Other people had also been starting to get fed up with her. Her new focus on being a good person transformed her relationships with everyone in her life.

Answering the Bell

There are many kinds of wake-up calls. Some come in a dream. Freddie was in his mid-thirties. He was a budding entrepreneur who hung out with a fast crowd of big spenders. On a trip to Los Angeles Freddie was at a party with hot-and-cold running hookers and a cocaine buffet. He overdosed, was taken to the hospital, and nearly died. An important deal fell through when news of this got out. His fiancée left him.

Why had this happened to him? he wondered. None of the other guys got in trouble, and some of them had done a lot more drugs.

One night after all this happened Freddie had a dream. He was a little boy walking into his grandfather's study. His grandfather was there surrounded by huge jars of candy. "Take whatever you want," his grandfather said. He woke up in tears.

Sometimes we just *know* what a dream means. Freddie knew. His grandfather had been dead for a number of years. He'd been a powerful, self-made man, a pillar of the community, a patriarch of the family. Freddie had been his favorite grandchild.

He felt the dream meant that he could become everything his grandfather had been: "Take whatever you want . . . of the good things I have." The key to the dream was the tears he shed when he woke up. They were tears of guilt and remorse over the stupid, wasteful things he'd done.

Now he understood that there was a reason why he got into such trouble. It was to remind him of the fact that the one thing he truly cared about was that one day he could become like his grandfather, a man of substance not because he was rich but because he was a good person. And if he didn't become a good person, he would never become a man of substance. Sometimes you don't see what you have until you come close to losing it.

There are many people like Freddie. Immaturity, distractions, living in the moment, laziness—all play a part in preventing these people from seeing how much they need to become good people. It often takes a disaster to reveal their destinies to them.

On Being Better Than You Think You Are

Let me tell you about Bradford. At twenty-nine, he was a big, solid, rugged-looking African-American. He owned a workshop where he made fine wooden furniture by hand. Dressed in brown corduroy pants and a black turtleneck, he looked uncomfortable talking about his life and his feelings.

Bradford had lived through one of those horrible childhoods that leave even old hands like me shaking their heads. It would've been a step up if his father had simply abandoned his family. But his father abandoned them, came back, spent their money, got drunk, beat up his mother, abandoned them again, and then came back again, restarting the whole process over and over. His mother coped by dragging Bradford and his sisters from one part of the city to another where she took dead-end jobs, got involved with cruel men, and drank to escape her pain.

Bradford had had to take care of his sisters. No one had ever taken care of him.

"I'm not here to complain," he said to me near the beginning of our work together. "It's just the opposite. My childhood is too much in my head and I want to get it out of my head. All it does is hurt me. I've screwed up every relationship I've been in. I'm afraid I'll never be able to open up or relax with anybody I care about. I feel like a car that was made in a really, really bad factory and all that car can think about is how he must be one really bad car. This is wrong and stupid. I want to stop feeling this way.

"What I keep asking myself is *Why did it happen to me, having a childhood like that?* I want to get the stuff from my past out of my life. I want to stop thinking about it. I want to get close to people. I want to stop feeling like a victim. I want to be happy. If I can just figure out some reason for what happened, I'll be okay."

"I'd like to ask you something, Brad," I said. "I know you went through some really tough times growing up. What do you think is the difference that made for you?"

"What do you want me to say? It sucked and it made me mad."

"Okay, that's good. Usually when we get mad we say, 'I'm gonna . . . *something.*' Well, in your case, what?"

"I was mad and I *didn't* want to do anything. I just wanted to make sure that I didn't do the same thing to my family when I have one. Sort of like, don't do unto others what you don't want them to do unto you, or something like that."

I took a deep breath. "Now I'm going to take a risk here. I'd be willing to bet that since you've grown up you haven't always been as good a person as you'd like to be."

Instead of getting insulted, Bradford agreed with me easily. "I don't actually get this, but I'm amazed at what a jerk I can be sometimes. I remember my father . . . if he was walking somewhere and you were in his way, he'd just shove you into a wall. I remember so clearly thinking I'd never be like that. But, no—if guys who work in my shop make a mistake, I can be brutal sometimes. I'm not trying to be mean. But then it's gradually dawned on me that maybe my father hadn't been trying to be mean either. Mean people just do it without trying. And I hate it so much when I'm a jerk like that. I couldn't feel worse."

"One more question, Brad. Has it ever caused you any real pain that you've mistreated someone?"

"That's what I just said," Bradford said sharply. "Weren't you even listening? I'd, like, cut down some guy who works with me and I could see he was hurt. You can tell because they avoid you for the rest of the day, like you're going to hurt them again. I'd see that and I knew I'd made it happen."

"Well, Brad, I have to tell you that you fit the pattern perfectly. I think I can show you right now a way for you to find meaning in what happened to you. What happened was to help you be a better person. More—to help you be a genuinely good person. Check it out. You were mistreated and that hurt you. You've mistreated others, and that not only hurt them, it also caused you pain as well. That means you're part of the club, the club of people who find meaning in what happened to them from the discovery that they need, really *need*, to become good people.

"Now you tell me," I continued. "Hasn't it been chewing you up inside to know that you want to be a good person, that you can be one, but to see that you're not really as good a person as you could be by far?" I was taking a risk. After all, he could say *no*.

Bradford stunned me. In a low voice he said, "I always thought of myself as a bad person. That's the truth. I was afraid I was like my father: bad like him and weak like my mother. I go around like, *Hey, I'm a good guy*, but that's a front. I don't want you to know the kind of person I'm afraid I really am."

"Maybe learning to be truly good can be something you take away from what happened to you because you have the capacity to be a much better person than you ever imagined. I just don't think really bad people think of themselves as bad. The fact that you thought that is a sign that you've always wanted to make the journey that you see in front of you."

"So what do I do now?"

Bradford's journey had begun.

After our work together I got a note from him. Here, in part, is what he wrote:

> Sometimes I still can't believe that what life had been trying to teach me was that I need to be a better person. I look at my hands that handle wood all day. Every day after work I put lotion on them to soften them up. Now I find out that the reason I went through the stuff in my life that I did was to soften me up and make me kinder and more compassionate.
>
> I don't think I would've come up with that reason in a million years on my own. You just get locked into the idea that tough things make you tough. All the craziness I went through growing up—hey, if you can't learn to take care of yourself, you're in trouble. I learned to take care of myself. I think I would've learned to take care of myself no matter what. That's the whole thing. I'm a tough guy. The reason stuff happened to me in my life wasn't to make me more of a tough guy. It was to help me

complete the picture, become a little softer, sweeter, kinder, hopefully easier to love one day.

I just want to thank you, Mira, for helping me with this.

As the letter continued I could see that Bradford went after his new life with his typical mixture of skepticism and practicality. He decided for the first time in his life he would become friends with women. He sensed that would help show him the way to become a better person.

One of the women he became friends with worked with teenage girls who were at risk. Bradford set up a program for teaching these girls carpentry skills. This woman had a five-year-old daughter. Eventually Bradford fell in love with this woman. They're now married, and he has adopted her daughter.

Hey, This Worked for Mother Teresa . . .

There we are in our busy, overcommitted lives. Suddenly we learn that everyone on the staff of Cosmic Kindergarten worked very hard to teach us that we need to become actively good. But how do you do that?

It's different for everyone, but the key is *doing something*—not waiting around thinking, but acting. If your neighbor's house was on fire, you wouldn't stand around wondering what was the best thing to do—you'd call the fire department, bring blankets for the people who've come out of the house, take in their pets so they don't have to worry about them, make coffee for the firefighters.

In the same way, if the meaning of what happened to you is that you need to be a good person, don't just stand there, *do something*. And always be thinking about doing something. For example:

- Think about something you care about, and do something about it.

- Think about a way you were hurt, and do something to help others who've been hurt the same way.

- The next time you're at a party, spot the loneliest-looking person there and talk to him or her.

- Imagine being your spouse. What do you think he or she needs to be just a little bit happier? Do that.

- Bring the kind of energy you have in life to being a better person. This is important——you just have to be a better you, not a different you. If you're in business, for example, look for opportunities for doing good the way you look for opportunities for making money. If your strong suit is one-on-one personal contact, then find ways to help people one-on-one.

- Don't feel sorry for yourself. It may feel that you have a steep road ahead of you, but it's a road that will give you a lot, and you're far from alone.

The history of the human race is filled with people who learned this lesson. We all know the story of Shakespeare's King Lear, a man with all the wealth and power a person could want, who makes a decision to retire. In the process he loses everything—not just his wealth and power, but the one daughter who truly loved him. But everything happens for a reason. For King Lear the reason was the necessary lesson of how to be kind. As a king he'd had everything. But he couldn't leave this earth until he'd learned to be a truly good person.

King Lear was one of those people who think of himself as a "winner," as if there were some inevitability to his successes. He may start to think that this inevitability comes from special talents or even from being chosen by God. With people like this you can often anticipate the coming disaster.

But success is never inevitable. People who believe they're winners get lazy, self-indulgent, arrogant. They're not good people, not as good as they could be. So when something bad happens, its meaning can be easy to read. They needed a lesson in how important it is to be a good person, with a particular focus on humility.

This is a very instructive point. Just think about it for a moment. Here we are living in Cosmic Kindergarten. Things happen to us to teach us lessons. The point of it all is learning. So maybe, just maybe, we can bypass the catastrophe by learning first. If we start out humble and stay that way, it's a little less likely that something will have to happen to teach us humility. After all, humble people work harder and don't take good outcomes for granted.

Postscript

Congratulations! You've had the gut sense that life, *your* life, is full of meaning. You were willing to take a big risk to find that meaning. *And now you've found it.*

I want to thank you for being the kind of person you are. All the good things in life come from people who have a deep conviction that everything that happens, everything they do, has meaning.

The fact that you've made this journey with me means you understand this. And now I think you also understand something else. Throughout our lives we're all reborn continuously as we repeatedly create new selves out of our encounters with life. Every time something happens that is big enough to shake us, whether it's bad or good, it fertilizes the self with some new learning that the self had somehow always been waiting for. And it's out of that that your new self is born.

Opportunities for this continuous renewal happen over and over. It's up to us whether we welcome this process and try to understand it. We can do that by being open to the fact that everything that happens to us has meaning and by looking for that meaning in the way I described in this book. If we do, Cosmic Kindergarten guarantees that all the good things that are possible for us, all the good things that can come from us, will in fact appear in our lives.

About the Author

In all my books they always say the same things about me. How I'm clinical director of The Chestnut Hill Institute in Boston. How I've written award-winning books. How I've been a therapist for thirty years now. This is all true, but it never quite feels like the real me.

Here are some things about me that do feel like me. My books are on serious topics but I'm basically a happy person, and I love to laugh and have fun. It must seem as if I know all the answers (after all, why bother writing a book if all you have are questions), but I have plenty of doubts, and the older I get, the more questions I have and the more open-minded I think I'm becoming. I know I can come across as very practical and hardheaded, and I am, but inside I feel very dreamy, and filled with dreams.

Also by Mira Kirshenbaum

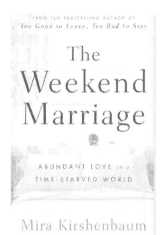

In this marriage guide for the twenty-first century, Mira Kirshenbaum shares the secrets of people who have figured out how to nurture their love no matter what their schedules.

The Weekend Marriage
1-4000-8098-3. $23.00 hardcover

Wherever books are sold

Harmony Books
CrownPublishing.com

Printed in the United States
by Baker & Taylor Publisher Services